D1523477

CRIMINAL JUSTICE

Prison and the Penal System

CRIMINAL JUSTICE

CRIMINAL JUSTICE

Prison and the Penal System

Michael Newton

CHELSEA HOUSE
PUBLISHERS
An imprint of Infobase Publishing

CRIMINAL JUSTICE: Prison and the Penal System

Chelsea House
An imprint of Infobase Publishing
132 West 31st Street
New York NY 10001

Library of Congress Cataloging-in-Publication Data

Newton, Michael, 1951–
Prison and the penal system / Michael Newton.
p. cm. — (Criminal justice)
Includes bibliographical references and index.
ISBN-13: 978-1-60413-893-1 (hardcover : alk. paper)
ISBN-10: 1-60413-893-9 (hardcover : alk. paper) 1. Prisons—United States History. 2. Imprisonment—United States—History. 3. Justice, Administration—United States—History. I. Title. II. Series.
HV9466.N49 2010
365'.973—dc22   2009048598

Text design by Erika K. Arroyo
Cover design by Keith Trego
Composition by EJB Publishing Services
Cover printed by Bang Printing, Brainerd, MN
Book printed and bound by Bang Printing, Brainerd, MN
Date printed: April 2010

Printed in the United States of America

10 9 8 7 6 5 4 3 2 1

This book is printed on acid-free paper.

All links and Web addresses were checked and verified to be correct at the time of publication. Because of the dynamic nature of the Web, some addresses and links may have changed since publication and may no longer be valid.

Contents

Introduction

Americans fear crime. Regardless of race, religion, or income, nearly all United States citizens agree that crime—whether committed by lone drug addicts, organized gangs, or fanatical terrorists—threatens the very fabric of civilized society.

Statistics provide ample grounds for that fear. In 2008, the latest year with full reports available, the Federal Bureau of Investigation (FBI) collected crime reports from 13,472 law enforcement agencies nationwide. Those reports document 16,272 murders; 89,000 forcible rapes; 441,855 violent robberies; 2,222,196 burglaries; 6,588,873 acts of larceny; 956,846 motor vehicle thefts; 62,807 cases of arson; 9,767,915 property crimes; and 834,885 aggravated assaults (involving serious physical injury). Offenders used firearms in 66.5 percent of the murders, 43.5 percent of the robberies, and 21.4 percent of the aggravated assaults. No statistics were collected for the use of weapons during rapes.[1]

On television programs such as *CSI, NCIS,* and *NUMB3RS,* police solve baffling crimes with the help of modern technology, capturing felons within 60 minutes (less time for commercials) and packing them off to prison. Few criminals escape, and those who do are nearly always jailed in later episodes.

Unfortunately, such is not the case with real-life crime in the United States.

Again, as reported by the FBI for 2008, police nationwide solved 63.6 percent of all reported murders, 39.3 percent of all rapes, 27.5 percent of known robberies, 11.6 percent of reported burglaries, 19.9 percent of known larceny cases, 12.3 percent of all motor vehicle thefts, 21.4 percent of arson cases, 17.4 percent of known property crimes, and 54 percent of aggravated assaults.[2]

Stated another way, the *unsolved* crimes for 2008 include 36.4 percent of all murders, 60.7 percent of all rapes, 72.5 percent of the robberies, 88.4 percent of the burglaries, 80.1 percent of the larcenies, 87.7 percent of all motor vehicle thefts, 78.6 percent of known arson cases, 82.6 percent of the property crimes, and 46 percent of all aggravated assaults.

From that perspective, there is good reason to feel unsafe in civilized America.

Some Americans react to that fear by arming themselves. According to the FBI, 7.7 million U.S. citizens purchased guns between January and September 2007, while 8.4 million more bought firearms during the same nine-month period in 2008.[3] No statistics exist for those who bought nonlethal weapons, guard dogs, home alarms, or who enrolled in martial arts classes for self-defense.

Others rely on law enforcement and the courts to protect them—a dangerous job for police, who saw 1,417 of their fellow officers killed on duty between January 2001 and early June 2009.[4] For many Americans, the solution to crime seems simple: more cops, more arrests, and longer prison terms for those convicted. Some would add a plea for swifter executions of criminals sentenced to die.

Politicians dependent on votes respond to those calls for relief from the grim plague of crime. In Congress, and in every state from coast to coast, lawmakers have increased spending on prisons, stiffened penalties for lawbreakers, and narrowed sentencing guidelines in pursuit of "zero tolerance" toward crime. Condemning crime and criminals is an approach that seldom fails to win approval on election day.

But does it work?

Modern America already jails more of its citizens than any other nation on the planet—one out of every 32 adults nationwide in 2007—yet crime rates remain fairly constant.[5] Clearly, the root problems, like so many American crimes each year, remain unsolved.

Prison and the Penal System examines America's methods of punishing crime, with equal time for the system's successes and failure. The book is divided into nine topical chapters.

Chapter 1, "Behind Bars," provides an overview of modern American penology, including recent statistics, definition of key terms, delineation of jurisdictions, and a brief introduction to major ongoing controversies.

Chapter 2, "Crime and Punishment," tracks the history of American penology from the colonial era to the 21st century, reviewing trends and techniques of handling convicted offenders.

Chapter 3, "Local Jails," charts the development of city and county correctional facilities, the offenses they punish, and various controversies surrounding their operations.

Chapter 4, "State Prisons," examines the historical growth of state prison systems, the criminals they confine, and controversial issues related to their methods.

Chapter 5, "Federal Prisons," traces the historical development of federal prisons, while comparing civilian and military penal systems.

Chapter 6, "Capital Punishment," covers the scope of capital crimes, methods of execution that have claimed an average 40 lives per year since 1608, and the ongoing debate over capital punishment in America.

Chapter 7, "Alternative Sentencing," surveys alternative forms of correction and the problem of repeat offenders.

Chapter 8, "Prison Rights and Wrongs," details the historical expansion of prisoner's legal rights, while discussing a broad range of penal problems and controversies.

Chapter 9, "New World Disorder," reviews the changes in American penology and prosecutions since the terrorist attacks of September 11, 2001, with prospects for the future.

Behind Bars

Atwater, California

Correctional officer Jose Rivera joined the Federal Bureau of Prisons in August 2007, after four years of service with the U.S. Navy that included two tours of duty in Iraq. His first assignment, at age 22, was the high-security prison for male inmates in Atwater, located on land once occupied by Castle Air Force Base, 130 miles southeast of San Francisco.

On the afternoon of June 20, 2008, Officer Rivera was locking cell doors in one of the prison's housing units, preparing for the daily 4:00 P.M. headcount. As he performed that task, inmates James Ninete Leon Guerrero and Joseph Cabrera Sablan attacked him, one of them wielding a crude knife made from parts of the prison cafeteria's dishwasher. Officer Rivera triggered his emergency body alarm, but none of the responding guards had keys to the cell block. They stood watching, helpless, waiting for a supervisor to produce the keys, while Guerrero and Sablan stabbed Officer Rivera 28 times, including a fatal wound to the heart.[1]

The killers—both from Guam, a U.S. territory in the Mariana Islands—had long histories of violence. Guerrero was suspected of killing corrections officer Douglas Mashburn in Guam, during 1987, but was not convicted in that case. In 1998 he received a life sentence for conspiracy to commit armed bank robbery. He arrived in Atwater one day before Officer Rivera's murder. Sablan, sentenced to life for murder and attempted murder on Guam in 1990, had been caged in Atwater since July 2005. He knew Guerrero from Guam, where the two were longtime jailhouse friends.

Investigation of Rivera's murder revealed that both killers were drunk when they attacked their latest victim. Homemade liquor was available to most inmates in Atwater, and parts from the same cafeteria dishwasher had been used to assault other guards in the past. Based on those findings, Rivera's family announced plans to file a wrongful-death lawsuit against the Federal Bureau of Prisons.[2]

Bryan Lowry, president of the Council of Prison Locals of the American Federation of Government Employees, questioned why the official report on Officer Rivera's death was not completed until April 2009 and

STGs

Prison gangs—known to law enforcement as *security threat groups* (STGs)—are criminal organizations formed inside prisons, whose members continue illegal activity in the "free world" when they are released. Most gangs recruit members of a specific race and may begin as a means of self-defense against other hostile ethnic groups, before they expand into drug-dealing, murder for hire, and other serious crimes. Prison administrators recognize six original (or "traditional") STGs. They include:

- The *Mexican Mafia,* formed in 1957 at the Deuel Vocational Institution in Tracy, California. Most members are *Sureños,* Mexican-Americans from Southern California.
- *La Nuestra Familia,* organized in 1965 at California's Soledad prison, by rival *Noreño* gangsters from northern California, known as mortal enemies of the Mexican Mafia.
- The *Black Guerilla Family,* a politicized African-American gang formed in 1966 by "Soledad Brother" George Jackson, later linked to the Black Panther Party and Black Liberation Army outside prison walls.
- The *Aryan Brotherhood,* a white racist gang founded in 1967 at California's San Quentin prison, later affiliated with outside groups such as the Ku Klux Klan and Aryan Nations.

was not released to the media for another two months. "It kind of makes you wonder why this thing took so long to come out," he said. "It's certainly not something to be proud of. For the most part, the control and supervision of inmates is still out of control. We're still drastically understaffed and our officers are still out there completely unarmed."[3]

A federal grand jury indicted Guerrero and Sablan for Officer Rivera's murder in August 2008. In March 2009 prosecutors announced their intention to seek the death penalty for both inmates, whenever their case goes to trial. Meanwhile, Warden Dennis Smith was transferred from Atwater to the medium-security federal prison in Pekin, Illinois, replaced by a warden from Kentucky.

- The *Texas Syndicate,* formed in the early 1970s by Mexican Americans from Texas, serving time in California prisons.
- The *Ñeta* ("New Birth") *Association,* formed at Puerto Rico's Oso Blanco prison in 1979, to fight the rival "G-27" gang, now linked to the violent Puerto Rican nationalist movement.

More recent, "nontraditional" STGs are also found from coast to coast. Arizona prisons harbor the Arizona Aryan Brotherhood, Arizona's Old Mexican Mafia, and Arizona's New Mexican Mafia. California has the Border Brothers, Bulldog Nation, 415s (affiliated with the Bloods street gang), and Nazi Low Riders. Los Solidos (the "Solid Ones") operate in Connecticut prisons. The New Mexico Syndicate, found in New Mexico's prisons, is an offshoot of La Nuestra Familia. New York City's jails host the Trinitarios, linked to various black and Hispanic street gangs. Texas seems overrun with STGs, including the Aryan Brotherhood of Texas, the Aryan Circle, Barrio Azteca, the Dirty White Boys, Hermanos de Pistoleros Latinos ("Brotherhood of Latin Gunmen"), the Mandingo Warriors, Mexikanemi ("Free Mexicans"), Texas Mafia, and the Tri-City Bombers.

Aside from criminal activity for profit, STGs pose a constant threat to nonaffiliated inmates and to prison personnel. Some require murder as a rite of initiation, and all have been linked to killings both inside and outside of prison.

PRISON NATION

In March 2008 a *New York Times* editorial referred to the United States as "Prison Nation."[4] That label surprised and outraged some readers who regard America in more traditional terms, as "the Land of the Free," but hard statistics support the critical tag.

In 2008 the International Centre for Prison Studies surveyed 215 countries worldwide and found that none imprisoned a higher percentage of citizens than the United States, with 756 out of every 100,000 residents incarcerated. Our neighbors in North America—Canada and Mexico—imprison 116 and 207 per 100,000, respectively. Overseas, Russia comes closest to the American rate, with 629 caged per 100,000. In Europe, Great Britain imprisons 153 per 100,000, while France jails 96 and Switzerland locks up 76.[5]

The real surprise comes from comparing the U.S. statistic to imprisonment in countries normally described by American media sources as "repressive" and "totalitarian." Cuba, condemned since 1959 for its harsh domestic policies, imprisons 531 persons per 100,000. Elsewhere in the dwindling communist realm, China jails 119 per 100,000 and Vietnam locks up 116. In war-torn Asia, Myanmar's military government jails 126 per 100,000, while Indonesia imprisons 58. Africa, infested with corrupt dictatorships, sees 22 per 100,000 jailed in the Congo, 36 in Sudan, and 28 in Nigeria. Even states ruled by strict Islamic law lag far behind America: 222 per 100,000 jailed in Iran, 209 in Libya, 132 in Saudi Arabia, 58 in Syria, and 55 in Pakistan.[6]

In human terms, those figures mean that 7.3 million Americans were either confined, on parole, or on probation in 2007—one out of every 32 adults nationwide. In June 2008 the Bureau of Justice Statistics found 2,310,984 prisoners held in local, state and federal lockups across America. Of those, 115,779 were women. A racial census of U.S. jails and prisons found 727 white male inmates per 100,000 males; 1,760 Hispanic males per 100,000; and 4,777 African American males per 100,000.[7]

Leading the world in imprisonment carries a heavy price tag. In 1987 the 50 states paid nearly $11 billion to house prisoners. By 2007 the cost had quadrupled to $44 billion. Five states—Connecticut, Delaware, Michigan, Oregon, and Vermont—spent as much or more on prisons as they did on higher education.[8]

WHAT'S IN A NAME?

Any discussion of prisons requires understanding of certain basic terms. Those used most commonly throughout this book include the following:

- *Penology,* from the Latin *poena* ("punishment"), is the science of prison administration and management. From the same root word, a *penal system* is the network of prisons within a particular area. *Penal codes* are laws that define specific crimes and dictate penalties.

- *Jail*—sometimes spelled *gaol* in Britain, Australia, and New Zealand—is a facility used to detain suspects before trial, and some persons convicted of *misdemeanors,* "minor" crimes with a sentence of one year or less. Most jails in the United States are local facilities, run by city or county authorities.

- A *prison* or *penitentiary* (from the Latin *pænitentia,* "repentance") is generally larger than a jail, used by state or federal authorities to confine persons convicted of crimes with a sentence exceeding one year. Most states maintain different prisons for violent and nonviolent offenders, ranked as having *minimum, medium,* or *maximum* security. So-called supermax prisons confine the most dangerous inmates or those with records of escapes from custody.

- *Capital punishment* refers to crimes for which convicted inmates may be executed (put to death).

- *Corporal punishment* involves physical punishment such as whipping or mutilation. Still popular in some foreign countries, corporal punishment is banned throughout the United States. Arkansas was the last state to abandon whipping, under federal court order, in the late 1960s.

- *Parole,* from the French *parole* ("spoken word"), refers to early release of convicted defendants based on their agreement to obey various regulations. Any violation may result in a return to prison.

- *Probation* is a sentence imposed by courts in lieu of incarceration. As with parole, defendants on probation must obey various rules and report periodically to supervisory officers.

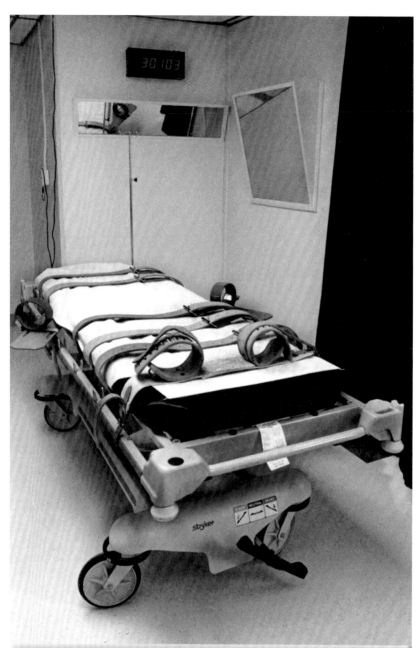

Lethal injection is generally believed to be more humane than death by firing squad, electric chair, and hanging. Many still argue, however, that the chemical cocktail amounts to cruel and unusual punishment, with some experts saying that poor training of death chamber workers complicates what should be an easy process. *AP Photo/Florida Department of Corrections, File*

○ *Home detention,* or "house arrest," is another alternative to incarceration. A convicted defendant's travel is strictly limited—if allowed at all—with exceptions generally restricted to work or school (in the case of juvenile offenders).

○ *Community service* is yet another form of alternative punishment, generally reserved for minor offenses and often tailored to make a specific impact—as when litterers are forced to pick up trash along highways, or celebrity drunk-drivers are compelled to make television commercials on the dangers of alcohol abuse.

○ *Fines* are monetary penalties imposed in place of, or in addition to, court-ordered terms of incarceration. Payments may include reimbursement to a defendant's victims for physical injuries and lost or damaged property.

WHO JAILS WHOM?

Arrests, trial, and punishment in the United States are governed by specific *jurisdictions,* from the Latin *iuris* ("law") and *dicere* ("to speak"). A jurisdiction is the geographic and/or political region controlled by a specific government. In America, jurisdictions may be local, state, or federal.

Local jurisdictions in the United States are further divided into *municipal* (city or town) and *county* jurisdictions (known as *boroughs* in Alaska and *parishes* in Louisiana). Large cities or towns maintain their own jails, courts, and law enforcement agencies, while smaller towns with limited budgets may rely on the county sheriff and jail to confine lawbreakers. In June 2008 local jails across America held 785,556 persons awaiting trial or serving a sentence, while another 72,852 were on probation or sentenced to community service.[9]

America's 50 *state* jurisdictions include at least one law enforcement agency for each state (most have several), with separate courts to try violators of state laws and various prisons established to confine them. In June 2008 a total of 1,409,442 convicted defendants fell under state jurisdiction, including those incarcerated and on parole or probation.[10] As of May 2009, 35 states permitted capital punishment, with 3,297 inmates under sentence of death, although two states—Kansas and New Hampshire—had executed no inmates since 1976.[11]

(continues on page 20)

MAD OR BAD?

All modern penal systems recognize the difference between "normal" offenders and those who are mentally ill, but standards for treatment differ from country to country, and even between jurisdictions within the United States. Many Americans believe that criminal defendants often plead "not guilty by reason of insanity" to escape punishment, when they are perfectly sane. In fact, such claims are relatively rare, and the courts resolve them with separate sanity hearings before trial begins.

Sanity and *insanity* are legal terms, with no meaning in medical science. The *irresistible impulse* rule, established by Ohio's courts in 1834, excused defendants whose mental illness forced them to act against their will or better judgment. In 1994 a Virginia jury used this rule to acquit Lorena Bobbitt of mutilating her husband after she learned of his affair with another woman.

The *M'Naghten Rule,* used by most British and American courts from 1843 to the 1950s, defined insanity as inability to recognize the difference between right and wrong. A person who shot his neighbor, believing that the victim was an invader from Mars, might still be convicted of murder if he—the shooter—understood that firing the shot was a crime.

The *Durham Rule,* established in 1954 by a U.S. Court of Appeals in Washington, D.C., exonerated defendants whose crimes resulted from a mental disease or defect. Psychiatrists were allowed to testify for both sides at trial, debating the suspect's mental condition and leaving the final decision to jurors.

The *Brawner Rule,* established by the same U.S. Court of Appeals in 1972, altered the Durham Rule, stating that a defendant may not be convicted if he "lacks substantial capacity to appreciate that his conduct is wrongful, or lacks substantial capacity to conform his conduct to the law."[12]

Many Americans were outraged in 1981, when John Hinckley shot President Ronald Reagan and was acquitted by jurors on grounds of *temporary insanity*. In 1984 Congress passed the Insanity Defense Reform Act, stating that a suspect should be acquitted only if "the defendant, as a result of a severe mental disease or defect, was unable to appreciate the nature and quality or the wrongfulness of his acts."[13] Critics complained that the new law essentially reverted to use of the old M'Naghten Rule.

Defendants acquitted on grounds of insanity normally are not released after trial. Despite a few rare cases where jurors deemed that a subject's temporary insanity had cured itself between commission of a crime and his or her trial, most "winners" in such cases are committed to mental hospitals for treatment, with the date of their release determined by psychiatrists. In jurisdictions that permit a verdict of "guilty but mentally ill," convicted defendants may receive psychiatric treatment to relieve their illness, *then* serve time in prison or on probation.

Three American states—Idaho, Montana, and Utah—have abolished all insanity defenses. Defendant Joe Cowan, sentenced to 60 years for attempted murder and burglary, challenged Montana's rule in 1994, but the U.S. Supreme Court upheld a state's right to ban insanity pleas.[14]

Five members of the jury which found John Hinckley Jr. not guilty by reason of insanity in the shooting of President Ronald Reagan testify before the Senate Judiciary Committee's Criminal Law subcommittee on Capitol Hill in June 1982. *AP Photo/Jeff Taylor*

(continued from page 17)

Federal jurisdiction spans the United States, plus its foreign territories and possessions, also including the U.S. armed forces. In June 2008 a total of 201,142 convicted defendants were under federal jurisdiction, either in prison, on parole, or on probation.[15] Both the U.S. government and its military branches practice capital punishment, although the military service has performed no executions since 1976. As of January 2009, a total of 55 federal inmates were held under sentence of death.[16]

DEBATING PUNISHMENT

Predictably, the punishment of criminals has sparked long-running controversy in America. Some punishments considered routine in colonial times were banned with adoption of the U.S. Constitution and its Bill of Rights, whose Eighth Amendment forbids "cruel and unusual punishments."[17] While that rule was ratified in 1791, the U.S. Supreme Court did not apply it to state prisons until 1947, in the case of *Louisiana ex rel. Francis v. Resweber,* and debate continues to this day over the proper definitions of "cruel" and "unusual," particularly in regard to capital punishment.

Discipline within prisons remains a persistent problem, aggravated by racial tension and organized gangs. While corporal punishment is banned by law nationwide, complaints of official brutality continue, requiring courts to judge individual guards and examine prison policies at large. Aside from physical security, the field of prisoners' rights includes First Amendment issues of free speech and religion, medical treatment, and disproportionate rates of incarceration based on race.

Juvenile justice has evolved from medieval times, when children might be hanged for theft, to a modern system including separate courts and prisons for minors. While some states ban execution of killers who commit their crimes before age 18, the U.S. Supreme Court ruled in 2002 that there is neither "a historical nor a modern societal consensus forbidding the imposition of Capital Punishment of any person who murders at 16 or 17 years of age." Two years later, the same court found that a "very immature" and "very impulsive" defendant should not be executed.[18] Nationwide, an increasing number of states favor incarceration of violent juveniles in adult prisons.

Sentencing of adult offenders also sparks controversy. While American judges historically have enjoyed wide latitude in sentencing, a trend toward *mandatory minimum sentences* began with New York's passage of a 1973 statute requiring a prison term of 15 years to life for anyone caught with more than four ounces of heroin or cocaine. Critics of that and other "zero tolerance" laws complain that relatively minor offenses may result in unfair sentencing, often influenced by a defendant's race or financial status.

Money definitely matters where justice is concerned, not only in deciding which defendants have the best attorneys, but also in terms of prison maintenance and operations. Since March 1984, when the Corrections Corporation of America built its Houston (Texas) Processing Center for the U.S. Immigration and Naturalization Service, privately owned jails and prisons, operated for financial profit, have multiplied across America. By December 2000 there were 153 private correctional facilities nationwide, with space for 119,000 inmates. That figure increased to 264 facilities by June 2003.[19] The same private prisons that save money for taxpayers have also spawned numerous scandals including charges of brutality, sexual abuse, and financial corruption.

There is no simple answer to the problems that surround modern prisons. Only education, close examination of the issues, and free debate can hope to solve those pressing issues as America's prison population increases each year, with no end in sight.

Crime and
Punishment

Columbus, Ohio

Built in 1834, with a capacity of 1,500 inmates, the Ohio State Penitentiary was habitually overcrowded. In April 1930 it housed 4,800 convicts—more than three times the number intended—and construction was in progress to expand the facility.[1] All work stopped on Easter Sunday, April 21, and the inmates of Sections G and H had just returned to their cells from dinner at 5:45 P.M., when a cry of "Fire!" rang out.

The blaze began in cellblock's northwest corner, where carpenters had built a wooden scaffold. The housing unit quickly filled with smoke. As the fire spread, inmates in other housing blocks began to riot, hurling stones at firefighters who came to douse the blaze.

Scenes of horror and heroism ensued. Two guards, William Baldwin and Tom Little, later testified that prisoners saved them from the fire after smoke left them unconscious. One prisoner carried 12 others to safety before he collapsed and died. Two inmates slashed their own throats to escape death by fire. When the smoke cleared at last, 320 inmates were dead, but only one had escaped, apparently disguised in civilian clothes.[2]

Multiple investigations revealed that Warden Preston Thomas had left a 71-year-old deputy in charge of the prison, while moonlighting at another job, and that no fire drills had ever been conducted. Officer Thomas Watkinson had refused to unlock any cells on the burning cellblock, prompting other guards to take his keys by force. The Columbus

Evening Dispatch placed blame for the fire "squarely upon the State," noting that lawmakers had "dawdled over the prison problem" for years without progress.[3]

Inmate James Raymond confessed to setting the fire, with two others, then hanged himself on August 21, 1930. Jurors convicted Hugh Gibbons and Clinton Grate of second-degree murder, and both received life sentences. Grate hanged himself in prison on January 15, 1935.[4] As a result of the disaster, Ohio established its first parole board in 1931. Over the next year, more than 2,300 inmates were released from the state penitentiary.[5]

LEGISLATING MORALS

From the voyages of Christopher Columbus onward, prisoners played a role in exploring and colonizing the New World. Spain and England both sent convicts westward as settlers, while enslaving Native Americans and later importing African slaves. In 1717 Britain's Parliament passed a law permitting courts to order "transportation" of noncapital offenders. Those who returned before their terms expired were hanged, along with anyone who helped convicts escape. By 1775 Britain had shipped more than 50,000 convicts to North America, with 5,000 dying in transit across the Atlantic Ocean.[6]

Most colonists considered themselves religious and moral people, adopting laws that echoed rules from the Old Testament. Acts such as adultery, blasphemy (insulting religion), criticizing clergymen, skipping church, and sodomy (homosexuality) were all serious crimes. Five colonies executed 10 defendants for sodomy between 1624 and 1674, while many others faced death for piracy, witchcraft, burglary, and theft. Three women were hanged in Massachusetts and Virginia for "concealing births." Slaves who rebelled were sometimes burned alive, and anyone who helped them might be hanged.[7]

For noncapital crimes, punishment often involved public humiliation. Adulterers wore a scarlet "A" on their clothes. Other defendants were locked in wooden frames called stocks or pillories, exposed to the weather while neighbors pelted them with rotten fruit. Some offenders were whipped or branded. Blasphemers were forced to stand on the gallows with a noose around their necks, simulating execution.

Prisoners work to clear away debris after a fire at Ohio State
Penitentiary in Columbus, Ohio on April 21, 1930. Over 300 inmates
were killed in the blaze. *AP Photo*

The colonies also had debtors' prisons for those who could not pay
their bills—a self-defeating system, since they earned no money in the
lockup—and jailed suspected witches prior to trial. Slaves were generally punished by their masters unless they rebelled, which was a capital
offense that claimed 72 lives in five colonies between 1710 and 1752.[8]

A NEW NATION

In 1776 the Declaration of Independence listed complaints against England's King George III (1738–1820), charging that he had "obstructed the Administration of Justice" by appointing biased judges, denying trial by jury, and "transporting us beyond Seas to be tried for pretended offences."[9] During the American Revolution (1775–1783), both sides held prisoners of war in makeshift prisons, including British prison ships. An estimated 11,500 colonial prisoners died aboard HMS *Jersey*, nearly three times the number of Americans killed in battle.[10]

American victory ended British transportation of convicts across the Atlantic, while the new United States debated handling of its prisoners and slaves. Some northern states banned slavery, while all passed new penal codes and converted colonial-era prisons to state service. Religious offenses were eliminated, but executions continued for a range of crimes, including murder, rape, burglary, robbery, forgery, horse theft, and slave rebellions.

Connecticut opened America's first state prison in 1790, while Philadelphia's Walnut Street Jail received its first prisoner that same year. Within a decade, new prisons stood in Georgia, Kentucky, Maryland, Massachusetts, New Hampshire, New Jersey, New York, Ohio, Vermont, and Virginia. The U.S. Constitution's Bill of Rights established basic guidelines for prosecution and punishment of crimes, but many years would pass before Congress and the Supreme Court extended those federal rights to state and local prisoners.

New York's Auburn Prison, built in 1816, segregated inmates on the basis of their crimes and introduced striped uniforms to make escapees obvious. Life at Auburn under the "congregate system" required inmates to work and eat together in strict silence, marching to and from their cells in lockstep—single file, with arms interlocked and heads bowed. Besides hard labor, each Auburn inmate was required to pray and meditate. "Industry, obedience and silence" were the rules imposed by Warden Elam Lynds, who transferred to Sing Sing prison in 1825.[11]

The founders of Pennsylvania's Eastern State Penitentiary, opened in 1829, proposed a different "solitary system," using one-man cells as a means to reform. Eastern State featured cells with skylights dubbed "windows of God," suggesting divine scrutiny of imprisoned sinners.

Other innovations included toilets and running water in each cell. British author Charles Dickens (1812–1870) deemed the solitary system "cruel and wrong" after touring the prison in 1842. He found "this slow and daily tampering with the mysteries of the brain, to be immeasurably worse than any torture of the body."[12]

Penal codes during this period favored "flat" sentences: specific terms of imprisonment for various offenses. The main goals of penology were punishment and isolation of convicted felons from society. In some states, "good time" laws permitted early release of model inmates, encouraging reform through hard work or, later, by volunteering as subjects for medical research. Still, discipline was harsh, and whipping was a common form of punishment.

WITCH TRIALS

Many early settlers believed in magic and witches, accepting the Old Testament's command that witches should be killed.[13] While published sources disagree on the number of witch trials held in colonial America, it is known that British colonists executed at least 34 supposed witches between 1647 and 1692. Many others were accused of witchcraft, facing lesser punishment or spending time in jail before they were acquitted. Other trials were held in New France (the area of North America controlled by France) and the area of present-day New Mexico, controlled by Spain until 1821.[14]

While Virginia staged the first known witch trial in 1622, no executions occurred until May 1647, when Achsah Young was hanged in Connecticut. Massachusetts authorities hanged Margaret Jones in June 1648 and executions continued through 1692, when the witch craze in Salem, Massachusetts, claimed 20 lives. The final death toll included 18 women and 16 men. Twenty-six were hanged in Massachusetts, seven in Connecticut, and one in Maryland.[15]

The Civil War (1861–1865) reintroduced military prisons to America's landscape. The Union held about 220,000 Confederate soldiers as prisoners of war, while the Confederacy jailed some 126,000 Yankees. Of those, 30,212 Union prisoners and 26,774 Confederate prisoners died in custody.[16] The most notorious wartime prison was Georgia's Andersonville. Built in February 1864 to house 10,000 prisoners, it was jammed with 32,000 by July and lost 100 men per day to disease and mistreatment—a total of 12,912 by April 1865.[17]

REFORM AND RESISTANCE

Emancipation of America's slaves shocked the South, where free labor supported the prewar economy and white supremacy was deemed a law

Although Massachusetts held the most witch trials (214), and Salem's panic is the most notorious from the colonial era, few colonies were spared entirely. Connecticut held 41 trials; Virginia, 23; Maryland, nine; New York, four; Carolina, Maine, and New Hampshire, two each; and New Jersey, one. New Mexico witnessed seven witch trials with multiple defendants, mostly Native Americans who refused to accept Christianity. All were enslaved for life.[18]

While no executions for witchcraft occurred in America after 1692, trials continued for another 186 years. Governor Thomas Velez Cachupin of New Mexico convened that colony's last witch trial in 1762, condemning several native tribesmen to slavery. Massachusetts held its last witch trial in 1878, with the defendant in that case acquitted.[19]

While witchcraft is no longer illegal in the United States and practitioners of Wicca—a neopagan, nature-based religion— are free to practice their "craft," many residents of other nations still fear black magic. In May 2008 rampaging mobs in the Kisii region of Kenya, East Africa, burned 11 suspected witches alive. Seven months later, a mob in Ecuador lynched two women suspected of witchcraft. Violent superstition persists.

of God. Fearing destruction of their social order, southern states passed "black codes" imposing harsh penalties on African Americans for various "crimes." Ex-slaves were banned from owning land or firearms and required to sign labor contracts with their former masters. Even public smoking was a crime in Alabama, where Black men could be whipped for lighting a cigar in public.

Most "black code" offenses were punished by fines, which ex-slaves could not afford to pay. Those without cash were jailed, and soon entered the convict lease system, which allowed county sheriffs to furnish inmate labor to wealthy planters and pocket the money. Thousands of African Americans fell prey to convict leases, sometimes "framed" for crimes they did not commit. Southern prison populations quickly increased: Georgia's grew tenfold between 1868 and 1908; Mississippi's quadrupled between 1871 and 1879; North Carolina's grew tenfold from 1870 to 1890; Florida's increased 850 percent from 1881 to 1904; Alabama's increased 650 percent between 1869 and 1919.[20]

While injustice flourished in the South, other states spawned a growing prison reform movement. Overcrowding, brutality, and the horrors of Civil War prisons prompted calls for change. In 1867 reformers Theodore Dwight and Enoch Wines complained, "There is no longer a state prison in America in which the reformation of convicts is the one supreme object of the discipline."[21] To solve that problem, Wines helped found the National Congress on Penitentiary and Reform Discipline in 1870, drafting a list of proposals for sanitary improvements, a ban on whipping and political appointment of wardens, broader education of inmates, and emphasis on reform instead of punishment.

New York's Elmira Reformatory, opened in July 1876, was the first prison to adopt those reforms. Warden Zebulon Brockway separated inmates into "grades," based on behavior, and offering vocational training with classes on ethics and religion. Whipping was banned, while recreational activities included an inmate band, newspaper, and athletic leagues. Unfortunately, New York's practice of indefinite sentencing caused tension among convicts who had no idea when they would be released, and Elmira reverted to corporal punishment that earned its warden the nickname "Paddler Brockway." In 1893 state investigators accused Brockway of "unlawful, unjust, cruel, brutal, inhuman, degrading excessive and unusual punishment of inmates, frequently causing permanent injuries and disfigurements," but he remained as warden until 1900.[22]

Meanwhile, in 1891, Congress passed the Three Prisons Act, authorizing construction of three federal lockups at Leavenworth, Kansas; Atlanta, Georgia; and McNeil Island, Washington. Construction began at Leavenworth in 1896, under Warden James French, with the first inmates arriving in 1897. Atlanta's federal prison opened in 1902. McNeil Island—which had housed prisoners since 1875—officially became a federal prison in 1904.

THE PROGRESSIVE ERA

America's Progressive Era (1900–1920) was an age of contradictions. It brought sweeping reforms in public health, labor and industry, women's suffrage, and protection of natural resources, but also witnessed U.S. military invasions of a dozen foreign countries, a ban on liquor that created a national crime syndicate, and proliferation of racism in the form of "Jim Crow" segregation laws, lynchings, and revival of the violent Ku Klux Klan.

Penology fell somewhere between the two extremes.

Warden Thomas Osborne took charge of New York's Auburn Prison in 1913 and began the process of reform. He banned whipping, lockstep marching, and mandatory silence, and established a form of inmate self-government called the Mutual Welfare League. Transferred to Sing Sing in December 1914, Osborne expanded his reforms and dramatically reduced inmate *recidivism* (returns to prison for new offenses). Political enemies forced his resignation in 1916 and reversed most of his improvements, sparking inmate riots in 1929.

Another aspect of "progressive" reform was the eugenics movement, pledged to improve the human race by weeding out genetic traits deemed undesirable. Early practitioners won support from President Theodore Roosevelt, the American Medical Association, and the National Academy of Sciences. Several states surgically sterilized convicts and other "undesirables"—including the mentally ill—between 1907 and 1942, when the U.S. Supreme Court's decision in *Skinner v. Oklahoma* ruled the practice unconstitutional. In some jurisdictions, eugenics also determined which inmates were granted parole.

WAR ON CRIME

"Crime waves" spawned by Prohibition (1920–1933) and the Great Depression (1929–1941) hardened American attitudes toward penology. Gang wars, high-profile ransom kidnappings, bank robberies, and soaring unemployment convinced many citizens that only harsh punishment—including frequent executions and life prison terms for repeat offenders—would make America safe.

PRIVATE PRISONS

California's San Quentin prison opened in July 1852 as a privately owned institution, but scandals later prompted state authorities to take control. Further experiments in penology for profit began in the South during Reconstruction (1865–76), when the convict lease system returned many African Americans to de facto slavery. Those programs rarely spread above the Mason-Dixon Line, however, and prisons nationwide were run by local, state, or federal governments until the early 1980s.

In 1983 a group of businessmen created the Corrections Corporation of America (CCA) to operate prisons for profit. Their first contract, in Texas, placed CCA in charge of a detention center for illegal aliens. By March 2009 the CCA ran 64 facilities, with 17,400 employees and 75,000 inmates. The firm reported profits of $150,940,000 in 2008.[23]

Other companies soon joined the penal gold rush, as various jurisdictions sought to reduce their expenses by hiring private contractors. CCA's competitors include Cornell Companies (with revenues of $386.72 million in 2008[24]), the Geo Group (formerly Wackenhut Security, revenues of $1.04 billion in 2008[25]), and Community Education Centers (specializing in treatment of "criminal and addictive behaviors"[26]). By 2007 there were 264 privately owned jails and prisons across the United States, housing 99,000 inmates.[27]

But while private prisons may save money for taxpayers, they also present major problems, including accusations of abuse. Some noteworthy cases include:

Between 1925 and 1939, America's incarceration rate jumped from 79 to 137 persons per 100,000 residents. As usual, minorities bore the brunt of that trend. Between 1930 and 1936, incarceration rates for African Americans tripled, while the rate for whites declined.[28] In the South, convict leasing continued, with flagrant corruption and brutality.

The federal government shared America's wish to get tough on crime. Congress created the Federal Bureau of Prisons in 1930, to

- *1997:* Guards at a private prison in Brazoria County, Texas, videotaped themselves beating inmates, shocking them with stun guns, and unleashing attack dogs on them. Investigation revealed that some of the guards were convicted felons.[29]
- *1999:* A lawsuit accused Geo Group prison guards of sexually abusing female inmates in Texas. Eleven guards and a case manager were indicted, while the company settled a civil lawsuit out of court for $1.5 million.[30]
- *2001:* Inmates of a Geo Group prison in Texas murdered a fellow inmate. Jurors awarded the victim's family $47.5 million for wrongful death.[31]
- *2004:* Inmate LeTisha Tapia committed suicide after telling relatives she had been raped and beaten by male inmates who shared her cellblock at a Geo Group prison in Texas. The company settled a lawsuit out of court for $200,000 in 2007.[32]
- *2005:* Jurors convicted three officials in Willacy County, Texas, of accepting bribes to approve prison contracts for developers Hale-Mills and Coplon.[33]
- *2006:* State authorities fined CCA $126,000 for short-staffing jails in two Colorado counties.[34]
- *2009:* Two Pennsylvania judges were convicted of accepting $2.6 million in bribes from Mid-Atlantic Youth Services, in return for sending 2,000 juveniles to the company's private detention facilities.[35]

Alcatraz was originally built as a Civil War fortress. It became the infamous federal prison in 1934. *Dave Etheridge-Barnes/Getty Images*

manage 11 existing facilities, then built three more before year's end, housing 13,000 inmates. By 1940 there were 24 federal prisons, with 24,360 inmates.[36] The most notorious was Alcatraz Island—"The Rock"—established in 1934 to house convicts including Chicago mobster Al Capone, kidnapper George "Machine Gun" Kelly, and members of the bank-robbing Barker-Karpis gang. Rip tides and hungry sharks in San Francisco Bay allegedly made Alcatraz escape proof.

Many prisons turned a profit for the government, using convict labor to manufacture goods for sale nationwide, but hardening attitudes cramped that trade in 1929, when the Hawes-Cooper Act permitted states to ban imports of prison-made products. The Ashurst-Sumners Act of 1935 tightened those restrictions, thus eliminating many prison jobs until the 1979 Percy Amendment allowed 37 jurisdictions to participate in joint "prison industry enhancement" programs.[37] Meanwhile, inmates in many state prisons fell idle, stripped of work programs that educated while relieving tension.

WINDS OF CHANGE

The public trials of Axis war criminals—coupled with domestic exposés such as *I Am a Fugitive from a Georgia Chain Gang,* published by escaped inmate Robert Elliott Burns in 1932—revived American support for prison reform after World War II, but serious change awaited the appointment of Earl Warren (1891–1974) as Chief Justice of the U.S. Supreme Court in 1953. Over the next 16 years, the "Warren Court" issued numerous rulings expanding the rights of minorities, criminal defendants, and those already convicted.

Defendants benefited from rulings in *Mapp v. Ohio* and *Katz v. United States* (limiting police searches), *Miranda v. Arizona* and *Escobedo v. Illinois* (requiring legal counsel during questioning), *Gideon v. Wainright* (providing lawyers for impoverished defendants), and *Terry v. Ohio* (requiring probable cause for arrests). *Tropp v. Dulles* barred the federal government from stripping convicts of their citizenship. *Monroe v. Pape* permitted state prison inmates to sue in federal court over denials of their civil rights.

As always, those gains produced hostile reactions. Conservatives branded the Warren Court "too liberal," complaining that it "handcuffed" police and turned prisons into "vacation resorts." While that was never true, events during the 1960s and 1970s pushed public opinion away from reform, back toward strict punishment of offenders. An image of chaos behind prison walls increased with the rise of violent gangs and a series of bloody riots: at San Quentin (six dead) and Attica, New York (43 killed) in 1971; at Oklahoma's state penitentiary (three dead) in 1973; and at New Mexico's (33 dead) in 1980.[38]

As American penologists increasingly rejected rehabilitation, a new "war on drugs" swelled state and federal prison populations. Harsh mandatory sentencing for possession of drugs, coupled with trials of juvenile offenders as adults, increased America's incarceration rate, and the conviction rate of nonwhites in particular. In 1972 an average of 162 American adults per 100,000 were imprisoned. That figure increased to 318 by 1984, and to 600 by 1995. A federal survey conducted in June 1994 found that 7 percent of all African-American men nationwide were in jail or prison, compared to 1 percent of white males. The majority of prison guards were white, and some were linked to racist groups such as the Ku Klux Klan.[39]

In such conditions, aggravated by the violence of prison gangs, would-be reformers view the future of American penology as bleak.

3

Local Jails

Crown Point, Indiana

Bandit John Dillinger (1903–1934) ranks among America's most notorious criminals of all time, often compared to 19th-century outlaw Jesse James (1847–1882). Dillinger's brief career as a bank robber included several escapes from custody and shootouts with police, none more dramatic than his breakout from the Lake County Jail on March 3, 1934.

Dillinger and other members of his gang had been captured in Arizona on January 25, and then returned to the Midwest for trial. Dillinger was sent to Crown Point, pending trial for the murder of police officer William O'Malley in East Chicago, while cronies Russell Clark, Charles Makley, and Harry Pierpont were sent to Ohio, facing trial for the slaying of Sheriff Jesse Sarber during a jailbreak at Lima. Those three were later convicted, but Dillinger did not intend to stand trial.

At 9:15 A.M. on March 3, Dillinger aimed an apparent pistol at jail handyman Sam Cahoon and ordered Cahoon to unlock his cell. Within minutes the bandit captured Warden Lou Baker, two deputies and a trusty (an inmate considered trustworthy by prison officials), seized two machine guns, and released inmate Herbert Youngblood, who was awaiting trial for murder. Dillinger and Youngblood escaped in a car owned by Sheriff Lillian Holley. They fled into Illinois, violating a federal law when they crossed the state line in a stolen vehicle. That offense put the FBI on Dillinger's trail and ultimately led to his death in Chicago, shot by federal agents on July 22, 1934. Herbert Youngblood did not last that long, dying on March 14 in a shootout that also claimed a deputy sheriff's life at Port Huron, Michigan.

Dillinger claimed that he escaped from Crown Point using a "gun" carved from wood and blackened with shoe polish, but many researchers doubt that colorful story. Skeptics claim that Dillinger's lawyer, Louis Piquette, delivered a real gun during a jailhouse visit to his client. Piquette was never charged with that offense, but he received a two-year prison term and a $10,000 fine in 1935, for harboring Dillinger gang member Homer Van Meter, who was not one of his clients. *Public Enemies,* a film starring actor Johnny Depp as Dillinger, premiered at Crown Point on June 30, 2009, one day before its nationwide release to theaters.

LOCAL LOCKUPS

In 2009 there were 19,429 recognized municipal (city) governments in the United States, plus 3,141 counties or county equivalents (called *boroughs* in Alaska and *parishes* in Louisiana).[1] All of the counties and many of the municipal jurisdictions maintain local jails. Some large and wealthy jurisdictions—such as Los Angeles, New York City, and Cook County, Illinois—have multiple lockups for suspects awaiting trial and inmates already convicted.

Local courts and jails deal with three kinds of laws. The first type, called *ordinances,* are local statutes restricted to a particular city or county, such as zoning laws, local traffic regulations, and curfews imposed on minors. Violation of an ordinance is an offense, rather than a crime, normally punished by monetary fines without incarceration. *Misdemeanor* statutes cover relatively minor crimes, rarely punished by incarceration except in cases of repeated violations. As a rule, the maximum sentence for a misdemeanor is one year in jail and misdemeanor records are often expunged (deleted) if convicted offenders maintain a period of good behavior after their release. The most serious crimes are *felonies,* punishable by incarceration in a state or federal prison for more than one year—including imposition of the death penalty for capital crimes. In olden times, all felonies rated execution, but current American law requires a homicide committed under "special circumstances."

Gangster John Dillinger, center, strikes a pose with Lake County prosecutor Robert Estill, left, in the jail at Crown Point, Indiana, in 1934. Dillinger escaped from the prison a few months later.
AP Photo

As of June 30, 2008—the most recent date with full statistics available—local jails in the United States housed 785,556 inmates awaiting trial or serving misdemeanor sentences, an increase from 780,174 in June 2007. Another 72,852 convicted defendants were under local jail supervision, serving sentences of probation or performing court-ordered community service as an alternative to incarceration. Nine percent of those—nearly one out of every 10—were non-U.S. citizens.[2]

The growth of America's local jail population in recent years has been alarming. In June 2008 one-third of all persons incarcerated nationwide were held in local lockups, 52 percent of those confined in America's 180 largest jail facilities. A total of 13.6 million persons were jailed during the 12 months ending on June 30, 2008. Meanwhile, the pace of trials had slowed, with 63 percent of those in jail awaiting trial, compared to 56 percent in 2000. Between 2000 and 2008, the number of jail inmates per 100,000 U.S. residents rose from 226 to 258.[3]

A federal survey of jail inmates in June 2008 revealed that 99 percent were adults (18 years or older), and 87 percent of those were males. In terms of race, 42.4 percent were white, 39.2 percent were African American, and 16.3 percent were Hispanic (with 2.2 percent listed as "other"). And while those figures indicate that a majority of prisoners in jail were white, comparison of racial populations tells a different story. Nationwide, 167 of every 100,000 whites were jailed, compared to 831 out of 100,000 African Americans, and 274 out of 100,000 Hispanics. In other words, African Americans, while comprising only 12.3 percent of America's total population, represent nearly 40 percent of those jailed.[4]

Racial disparities are even more extreme for women held in U.S. jails. Females comprise 50.7 percent of America's population but only 13 percent of adult jail inmates. Within that small group, African-American women have an incarceration rate of 349 per 100,000—twice as frequent as Hispanic females (at 147 per 100,000), and 3.5 times more frequent than white women (at 93 per 100,000). Nationwide, the number of incarcerated women grew by 33 percent between June 2000 and June 2008.[5]

LIFE INSIDE

It comes as no surprise that housing of suspected and convicted criminals presents a wide range of serious problems for those in charge of America's jails. Individual cities and counties rarely publish statistics concerning jailhouse problems—in fact, some stand accused of illegally concealing them—and while the Bureau of Justice Statistics varies its focus from one year to the next, available reports suggest the scope of difficulties faced in local jails. The federal Death in Custody Reporting Act of 2000 also provides more detailed information on jailhouse fatalities.

Homicide in jails, whether committed by gangs or resulting from individual feuds, claimed 147 lives nationwide between 2000 and 2006 (the last year with statistics presently available). Of those killed by fellow inmates, 144 were male and three were female; 59 were white, 59 were African American, 27 were Hispanic, and one was recorded as "other." Only one of those slain was below age 18.[6]

(continues on page 40)

COOK COUNTY JAIL

Illinois lawmakers created Cook County in January 1831, when Chicago—the county seat—had less than 60 residents. Crime was so rare that the first jail, resembling a frontier stockade, was not built until 1835. A larger jail opened in 1852, but it was destroyed by the Great Chicago Fire in October 1871. Reopened as the Chicago House of Corrections, the new jail housed an average 419 inmates per day, including some children as young as seven.[7]

By the 1920s, when Prohibition and its gang wars brought global notoriety to Chicago, the county jail housed 1,200 inmates, more than twice its capacity. Expansion in 1928 failed to keep pace with bookings—an average of 3,200 inmates—but wealthy gangsters such as Al Capone and Frank "The Enforcer" Nitti still rated spacious cells, luxurious furniture, and gourmet meals, provoking public scandals.[8]

In the 1950s Cook County's jail served as a local mini-prison for convicted felons, with its own electric chair where executions were performed. In 1954 some 60 percent of its inmates were serving sentences up to five years. The state responded slowly to worsening conditions, but a new law passed in 1969 created the Cook County Department of Corrections, paving the way for construction of 11 jail facilities, which presently house 10,000 inmates, supervised by a staff of 3,800.[9]

Despite those improvements, problems continue. In July 2008 the U.S. Department of Justice's Civil Rights Division published a report declaring that Cook County had systematically violated the Eighth Amendment's ban on cruel and unusual punishment, failing to protect inmates from violence, prevent suicides, or to provide sanitary living conditions required by law. Specific violations included frequent beatings of inmates by guards; unhealthy food; overcrowding that forced many inmates to sleep on cell floors; rodent infestation resulting in numerous rat bites; violations of privacy during repeated invasive strip searches and painful medical examinations; failure to dispense prescribed medications; and long delays in releasing prisoners on bail, when their sentences were finished, or when charges had been dropped. One inmate's leg was amputated in 2006, after jail staff left an infection untreated. During the same year, a female inmate died from lack of medical attention in the county jail.[10]

Cook County Sheriff Thomas Dart complained that the federal report "often relies on inflammatory language and draws conclusions based on anecdotes and hearsay from inmates," adding that the "allegations of systematic violations of civil rights at the jail are categorically rejected by the sheriff's office." Nonetheless, a federal court awarded jail inmates an average $1,200 each in damages for mistreatment suffered at the Cook County Jail.[11]

Cook County Jail in Chicago, the nation's largest single-site county jail, has a history of serious sanitation and medical care problems as well as violence against prisoners who clashed with guards or failed to follow commands. *AP Photo/Jeff Robertson, File*

(continued from page 37)

Depression and mental instability may explain the 2,706 inmate suicides reported between 2000 and 2006. Those who killed themselves included 1,912 males and 163 females; 1,441 were white, 306

BRIAN GENE NICHOLS

Brian Nichols was born to a middle-class Maryland family in December 1971 and graduated from high school in Baltimore at age 18. He attended Pennsylvania's Kutztown University for three semesters during 1989–1990, where his size and martial-arts skills made him a tough linebacker on the school's football team. Nichols also logged three arrests during his Kutztown tenure, including charges of assault, disorderly conduct, criminal mischief, criminal trespass, harassment, and making terroristic threats. Police dropped the charges in each case, and Nichols transferred to Newberry College, in South Carolina, for the 1992–1993 school year. He played more football at Newberry until theft charges got him kicked off the team, and then he dropped out of school.

Nichols moved to Atlanta, Georgia, in 1995, working as a computer engineer for Hewlett-Packard (1995–2004), and then shifting to a similar position with the United Parcel Service. That job ended in September 2004, when Nichols was arrested for raping an ex-girlfriend at gunpoint. Charged with multiple felonies, he faced a potential life sentence, but jurors failed to reach a verdict at his first trial. When told that prosecutors would try him again, Nichols warned, "I'm not going to go lying down."[12]

Friends and relatives, including his mother, warned authorities that Nichols planned a jailbreak. While escorting Nichols to his second trial on March 10, 2005, officers found two homemade knives in his shoes. Judge Roland Barnes requested extra security, but when Nichols returned to the Fulton County Justice Tower on March 11, he was guarded by a single deputy: Cynthia Hall, who stood 12 inches shorter than Nichols. When Hall released Nichols from his chains, permitting him to were African American, 254 were Hispanic, and 70 were "other." A higher number of minors—32, or 1.2 percent of the total—chose to end their own lives. Federal surveys reveal that the suicide rate in

change from jail garb to civilian clothes, Nichols knocked her unconscious and took her gun belt, including extra ammunition and a police radio.

Deputy Hall survived that attack with brain damage, but others were less fortunate. Invading the judge's chambers, Nichols seized three hostages and demanded to see Judge Barnes. Next, Nichols confronted a bailiff and took his pistol, as well. Entering Judge Barnes's courtroom with a trial in progress, Nichols shot Barnes in the head, killing him instantly, then fatally wounded court stenographer Julie Brandau. Fleeing the courthouse, Nichols shot and killed a sheriff's deputy, Sergeant Hoyt Teasley, who tried to stop him. Nichols then ran to a nearby parking garage and stole a car belonging to Deputy Solicitor General Duane Cooper.

A court employee followed Nichols to another parking garage and alerted police to his location, but Nichols hijacked a second car, then fled to a third parking garage where he commandeered yet another vehicle. He then drove to Centennial Tower, next-door to CNN News headquarters, and stole a fourth car, pistol-whipping its owner. Nichols killed his last victim, U.S. Immigration and Customs Enforcement agent David Wilhelm, at home in Atlanta, stealing a handful of change.

The search for Nichols ended on March 12, after he invaded an apartment in Duluth, Georgia, and held its occupant hostage. The tenant cooked breakfast for Nichols and gave him drugs that lulled him prior to capture by Atlanta SWAT officers. Charged with 54 felonies related to his escape, Nichols was convicted on November 7, 2008, and received multiple life sentences without parole. Concerning his escape, attorney John Matteson blamed short-staffing at the courthouse. "They just don't have the manpower to deal with it," he said. "They're good folks, but they're pushed to the limit."[13]

local jails is triple the rate for state prison inmates, and that violent offenders are twice as likely to kill themselves as are those charged with nonviolent crimes.[14]

Another form of jailhouse violence—sexual victimization—is not as fully documented. The Prison Rape Elimination Act of 2003 requires the federal government to collect statistics on sexual assaults in custody, but reporting by state and local jurisdictions remains incomplete. A total of 352 local jails nationwide reported 3,084 sexual assaults during 2004–2005, with 336 attacks resulting in the victim's death. Most of those cases involved assaults by inmates, but prisoners also reported attacks by guards, including 2.5 percent of all cases reported in 2004 and 1.4 percent in 2005.[15]

Health problems unrelated to violence—both physical and mental—are a major problem in America's jails. A federal survey of local jail inmates conducted in 2002 found more than one-third claiming medical problems, while 22 percent claimed learning disabilities, and 11 percent had poor vision. An average 290 inmates per 100,000 were diagnosed with serious heart problems. One-fourth of those with mental health problems had been jailed three or more times for various offenses.[16]

Health problems pose a threat to life in jail, where medical treatment may be of poor quality. Between 2000 and 2006, 368 local jail inmates died from AIDS, while another 3,311 died from other unspecified ailments. Deaths from illness overall claimed the lives of 3,223 male inmates and 456 females; 1,522 were white, 1,642 were African American, 436 were Hispanic, and 64 were "others." Six of those who died were under the age of 18.[17]

Many Americans are arrested for crimes committed while they are intoxicated by alcohol or illegal drugs, and their addiction follows them to jail. The federal survey conducted in 2002 found 68 percent of jail inmates admitting substance abuse prior to arrest, while 16 percent committed their crimes to get money for drugs. Drug or alcohol intoxication *inside* jail claimed 489 lives during 2000–2006, including 386 male inmates and 103 females. Of those, 295 were white, 119 were African American, 64 were Hispanic, and eight were "other." Two of the dead were minors.[18]

An observation window in the Montague County jail is obstructed by inmates. Such conditions, in addition to misconduct on the part of the guards and the sheriff, led to the jail being shut down in January 2009. *AP Photo*

SCANDAL!

Most Americans are happy to forget that jails exist, until news of some scandal behind bars reminds them, embarrassing local officials and prompting new calls for reform. Some recent cases include

- *April 2006*: Two sheriff's deputies resigned after exposure of their sexual activities with female inmates at the aptly named Purgatory Jail in Washington County, Utah. Sheriff Kirk Smith told reporters that his investigation of those "inappropriate relationships" had revealed "several other things that were not directly related to the investigation itself and in violation of departmental policy," including delivery of unauthorized gifts to inmates by their guards.[19]

- *October 2006*: Two officers at Pennsylvania's Monroe County Correctional Facility resigned after their sexual relationships with inmates were exposed. Two more were suspended in December, on identical charges, and later resigned. In March 2007 six corrections officers and a female kitchen employee were indicted for various crimes. Warden David Keenhold resigned in May 2007 but denied that his decision had anything to do with the ongoing scandal. In June 2007 a seventh guard was charged with passing contraband to inmates. Between that date and January 2008, six officers pled guilty to various charges. Only one received jail time, while the rest were sentenced to probation. Authorities suspended the jail's new warden and a captain of the guards in March 2009, during a fresh investigation. Yet another guard was fired in May 2009, for failure to make his rounds while an inmate committed suicide.[20]

- *February 2009*: A Texas grand jury indicted 17 defendants in a scandal at the Montague County jail. Most were former guards, including several women, accused of having sex with inmates and providing them with cell phones or illegal drugs. Two inmates also faced charges of drug possession. Ex-sheriff Bill Keating, indicted with the rest, had already pled guilty in federal court to sexually assaulting a female inmate. Keating died on May 1, 2009, while awaiting his sentence in that case.[21]

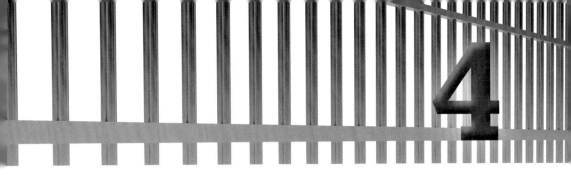

State Prisons

Columbus, Ohio

While bandit John Dillinger escaped from Indiana's Crown Point jail on March 3, 1934, other members of his gang were not so lucky. Russell Clark, Charles Makley, and Harry Pierpont stood trial for the October 1933 murder of Sheriff Jesse Sarber in Allen County, Ohio, and all three were convicted. Three weeks after Dillinger's last jailbreak, on March 24, Makley and Pierpont were sentenced to die, while Clark received a life prison term.

News of Dillinger's death in Chicago, shot by FBI agents on July 22, 1934, shocked his imprisoned cronies. Two months later, on September 22, Makley and Pierpont tried to escape from death row at Ohio's state prison in Columbus. Armed with "guns" carved from soap and blackened with shoe polish, the killers got out of their cells, but found their exit barred by more locked doors. Guards armed with rifles killed Makley and wounded Pierpont in the head and spine. A prison doctor kept Pierpont alive long enough for his walk to the electric chair, on October 17, 1934.

Russell Clark, who took no part in the failed prison break, served 34 years at Columbus before his parole on August 14, 1968. The world had passed him by, and he had only weeks left to live. Cancer claimed his life on Christmas Eve.

DISUNITED STATES

Each of America's 50 states maintains a prison (or "corrections") system established and maintained in accordance with state law. All states have multiple prisons, but no reliable census exists for the total number of state prisons nationwide. At the time of this writing, Alabama had 24, Alaska had 14, California had 44 (33 for adults, 11 for juvenile offenders), and so on.[1] Hawaii is unusual: Aside from four prisons, state officials also run Hawaii's four jails, one each on the islands of Hawaii, Kauai, Maui, and Oahu.[2]

On June 30, 2008, the Bureau of Justice Statistics found 1,409,442 inmates confined to state prisons nationwide. Thirty-four states reported increases in their prison populations for the first six months of 2008, while 16 reported a decline. States with the largest growth rate included Minnesota (5.2 percent), Maine (4.6 percent), Rhode Island, and South Carolina (both up 4.3 percent).[3]

State prisons normally confine inmates convicted of felonies; those are crimes punished by terms exceeding one year, including life terms (with or without parole) and death sentences in states that practice capital punishment. Sometimes, "problem" prisoners are transferred from one state's prison system to another, generally to separate them from criminal cohorts or to protect them from inmates who may seek to harm them.

Felony sentencing has never been consistent among the 50 states. Before World War II, some states imposed life terms—and occasional death sentences—on repeat offenders judged to be habitual criminals. Interpretations of "life" sentences and "good time"—time deducted from an inmate's sentence for "good behavior," or simply to relieve crowded prisons—vary widely across the country. Since 1993 several states have passed "three-strikes" laws to imprison three-time felony offenders for life, while many other jurisdictions have adopted mandatory sentences for specific violent or drug-related crimes. A popular but inconsistent "truth in sentencing" movement also seeks to limit the release of felons on parole, demanding that they serve the full sentence imposed at trial.

SECURITY LEVELS

All states maintain prisons tailored for inmates of varied backgrounds and potential danger to society, or to those assigned to guard them.

While various states adopt different labels, the basic levels of prison security are generally called minimum, medium, maximum, and supermax.

Minimum security prisons confine the least dangerous offenders and those least likely to escape. Most corporate or "white-collar" criminals fall in this category, a fact that breeds complaints of wealthy, mostly white inmates receiving favored treatment from the state. Some critics describe minimum security prisons as "country clubs." Inmates from these facilities are frequent candidates for work-release programs granting part-time access to the outside free world.

Medium security prisons often include dormitories (locked at night) rather than individual cells, with communal bathroom facilities, lockers for personal possessions, and other amenities, but their double fences and routine patrols by uniformed guards set them apart from the more relaxed atmosphere of minimum security lockups.

Maximum security prisons typically have fortress-like walls with armed guards in watchtowers, one- or two-inmate cells with barred sliding doors controlled from a central guard station, and strict supervision of all inmate movements to work stations, dining halls, showers, or the exercise yard. Electrified fences—including some with lethal voltage—are often employed. In capital punishment states, death row is normally patrolled under even tighter security, with condemned inmates confined to individual cells for most of each day.

Supermax prisons are designed to hold the most violent and/or notorious inmates, including serial killers and rapists, terrorists, and members of organized crime. Strict rules of confinement and limitation of visiting rights theoretically prevent gangsters and other "public enemies" from communicating with accomplices still at large. Supermax inmates and civil libertarians often complain that the terms of confinement amount to unconstitutional "cruel and unusual" punishment, but American courts have upheld the legality of supermax solitary confinement.

LIFE AND DEATH INSIDE

It comes as no surprise that state prisons witness more violence than local jails. Between 2001 and 2006, eight correctional officers were slain

GEORGE JACKSON (1941–1971)

A Chicagoan who moved to California as a child, George Jackson spent time in the California Youth Authority for juvenile offenses before he was convicted of robbing a gas station at age 18. While confined at San Quentin, in 1966, he founded the Black Guerrilla Family as a Marxist political group. He later joined the militant Black Panther Party and began corresponding with Angela Davis, a controversial college professor and Communist Party member. Authorities soon moved Jackson to Soledad Prison, scene of many racial confrontations.

In January 1970, after Soledad guard O.G. Miller shot and killed three African-American inmates involved in a fight, another guard—John Mills—was thrown from an upper cellblock tier to his death. Authorities indicted Jackson, John Cluchette, and Fleeta Drumgo for killing Officer Mills. Returned to San Quentin and solitary confinement, Jackson began writing a book, *Blood in My Eye,* which described his life in prison.

On August 7, 1970, Jackson's younger brother Jonathan helped three San Quentin prisoners escape from the Marin County courthouse at gunpoint, sparking a shootout that left Jon Jackson, Judge Harold Barnes, and two of the inmates dead. Police traced Jon Jackson's guns to purchaser Angela Davis,

by inmates in six states.[4] During the same years, according to statistics collected under the Death in Custody Reporting Act, 18,550 inmates died in various adult state prisons. Of those, 299 were murdered, 1,172 committed suicide, 213 died from alcohol or drug intoxication, 180 suffered fatal accidents, 16,489 died from various diseases, and the cause of death in 197 cases remains officially "unknown."[5]

Death statistics for state prisons mirror those for local jails, in terms of sex and race. Murder victims for 2001–2006 included 296 males and three females, while 1,138 men and 58 women took their own lives. Deaths from intoxication were equally unbalanced, including 207 men and six women. Nine of those reported dead in adult prisons were minors—including one murder victim and two suicides—but a separate who employed him as a bodyguard. FBI agents charged Davis as an accomplice to the killings, but jurors acquitted her of all charges in June 1972.

Meanwhile, three days before his scheduled trial in the Mills murder—on August 21, 1971—George Jackson received a visit from attorney Stephen Bingham at San Quentin. Guards later claimed that Jackson returned from the meeting wearing an Afro wig that concealed a large handgun, allegedly smuggled into the prison by Bingham. Jackson reportedly used the gun to seize control of his cellblock, starting a riot that claimed his own life, plus those of three guards and two other inmates. Jackson's supporters still say he was "set up" and murdered by prison authorities, a claim supported by state police informant Louis Tackwood in sworn testimony and a book, *The Glass House Tapes* (1973).

Before Jackson's death, a collection of his prison letters was published under the title of *Soledad Brother* (1970). *Blood in My Eye* became a best-seller in 1972, and its popularity increased when jurors acquitted John Cluchette and Fleeta Drumgo of killing Officer Mills. Stephen Bingham fled America and spent 13 years in Europe, then returned in 1984 to face trial for his alleged role in the San Quentin riot. Jurors found him innocent of all charges in July 1986.

count was reported for deaths in state juvenile prisons, with 43 fatalities reported during 2002–2005. Those deaths involved 38 boys and five girls, including five homicides, 17 suicides, two fatal accidents, 10 deaths from illness, and five with "unknown" causes. The most dangerous states for inmates were California (with 81 murders), Texas (22), Maryland (16), Florida, and Oklahoma (15 each).[6]

As in local jails, while white prisoners comprise a majority of those confined, the percentage of nonwhites imprisoned—and those who die in custody—is disproportionate to their numbers in America at large. In June 2008 state prisons housed 727 white male inmates per 100,000 white men nationwide, compared to 4,777 African-American males per 100,000 and 1,760 Hispanic males per 100,000. African Americans, comprising

12.3 percent of America's population, represented 33.8 percent of all state prison inmates murdered, 21.5 percent of those who committed suicide, and 19.7 percent of those who died from alcohol or drug intoxication. Hispanics, with 12.5 percent of the total U.S. population, represented 18.7 percent of murdered state prisoners, 16.8 percent of prison suicides, and 17.4 percent of deaths from banned intoxicants.[7]

JUVENILE JUSTICE

In old Europe and colonial America, children suffered adult punishment for felonies, including public execution in some cases. American handling of juvenile offenders began to change in 1824, when New York opened a House of Refuge for young criminals deemed reformable. Michigan followed suit in 1855, with its House of Corrections for Juvenile Offenders in Lansing. Illinois created the nation's first juvenile court in 1888, with passage of "An Act to Regulate the Treatment and Control of Dependent, Neglected and Delinquent Children." Still, another 79 years passed before the U.S. Supreme Court's ruling in an Arizona case *In re Gault*, 387 U.S. 1 (1967) extended the full rights of adult defendants to minors, in 1967.[8]

Many juvenile defendants are classified as status offenders—violators of laws that apply only to persons of a certain status, in this case their age. Those offenses typically include possession of alcohol, firearms, or other items forbidden to minors; driving below legal age; violation of curfews; truancy from school; and so forth. Federal sentencing guidelines define juvenile status offenses as crimes which cannot be committed by adults.

America has no unified system of juvenile justice. Rather, it has 51—the several states, plus Washington, D.C. Various states are free to set the ages they prefer for drinking, driving, sexual consent, and so on, although the National Minimum Drinking Age Act of 1984 permits denial of federal highway funds to states that permit persons below age 21 to drink alcoholic beverages.

While Congress and the FBI have issued warnings against "juvenile delinquents" since the 1950s, fear caused by juvenile crime only peaked in the closing decades of the 20th century. From 1988 onward, various state legislatures passed laws excluding violent young offenders from trial in juvenile courts, permitting more to be tried as adults and confined to state prisons.

While that campaign won votes for conservative lawmakers, it had no apparent impact on juvenile crime rates. In 2007 alone, juvenile offenders were involved in 12 percent of America's violent crimes and 18 percent of all property crimes cleared by police. Eleven percent of all American murder victims were below age 18, and 35 percent of those victims were under age five. Nationwide, arrests for homicide jailed 4.1 out of every 100,000 minors aged 10 to 17, a 24 percent increase since 2004. African Americans accounted for 17 percent of all juveniles in that age range, but they comprised 51 percent of those jailed for violent crimes and 32 percent of juveniles arrested for property crimes.[9]

FAMOUS LOCKUPS

America's most famous—or infamous—state prisons include the following institutions, each an enduring part of penal history.

Sing Sing Correctional Facility

This was one of two state prisons authorized by New York lawmakers in 1796. The first, at Auburn, opened in 1816, while work on the second—at Ossining, named for the Sinck Sinck tribe that once occupied its site—was built by Warden Elam Lynds in 1825. Using the "Auburn system"—including strict silence and frequent whippings of troublesome inmates—Lynds created a "model prison" that turned a profit for New York. Lynds retired in 1830, during an investigation sparked by a female inmate's pregnancy, and conditions at Sing Sing swiftly declined. Rampant disease and fires climaxed with a riot in 1861, suppressed by the militia. Conditions were chaotic when Warden Lewis Lawes took command in 1920: One head-count found 53 of 897 inmates missing, while another convict had served five years with no record of his entering the prison. Lawes instituted various reforms, modernizing the prison before he retired in 1940. Today, Sing Sing houses 1,700 inmates and its original cellblock is scheduled to become a museum.[10]

The roofless, original, stone Sing Sing prison cell block, now scheduled to become a museum, sits in the middle of the present-day maximum security prison in Ossining, New York. *AP Photo/ Jim McKnight, File*

Eastern State Penitentiary

Located in Philadelphia, Eastern State received its first prisoners in 1829. Established as a model of reform, it inspired construction of 300 "enlightened" prisons later built throughout South America, Europe, the British Empire, China, and Japan. The prison's design, by architect John Haviland, made it a popular tourist attraction, but Eastern State's scheme of solitary meditation failed to reform prisoners. Warden Michael Cassidy built traditional cellblocks during the 1870s, a congregate workshop opened in 1905, and the "solitary system" was totally abandoned by 1913. Construction continued through 1956, with completion of death row on Cellblock 15. Eastern State closed forever in 1971, but the massive structure still stands. It is rumored to be haunted and has been featured in several episodes of the Sci-Fi Channel's *Ghost Hunters* series.[11]

Texas State Penitentiary at Huntsville

Also known as "The Walls," this was the Lone Star State's first enclosed prison. Huntsville received its first inmates in October 1849. Four years

THOMAS MURTON (1928-1990)

Before turning to penology, Tom Murton earned a degree in animal husbandry from Oklahoma State University (1950) and another in mathematics from the University of Alaska (1958). He obtained a master's degree in criminology from the University of California in 1964 and fulfilled requirements for a Ph.D. in the same subject two years later.

In 1967, while teaching at Southern Illinois University, Murton was hired to reform the scandal-ridden Arkansas prison system. The state's two prison farms, at Cummins and Tucker, still used whipping to punish inmates, and Murton found that other forms of torture—including electric shocks from a hand-cranked telephone—were common. Aside from rampant brutality, Arkansas prisons were also mired in corruption that seemed to involve state officials. Employment of violent inmates as guards produced unbearable conditions, aggravated by poor housing, food, and medical care.

Murton lost official support in Arkansas as he exposed corruption and discovered unmarked graves around the Cummins prison farm, suggesting that inmates—some found with their legs cut off to fit undersized coffins—were murdered and secretly buried. State authorities fired Murton in 1968 and closed the investigation, which Governor Winthrop Rockefeller called "a sideshow." Claims persist that another 200 graves remain unopened at the farm. Murton returned to teaching after Arkansas authorities spread tales of his unfitness to serve in other prison systems.[12]

In 1980 Murton retired to farming, near his hometown of Deer Creek, Oklahoma. He also published two books on prison reform: *Accomplices to the Crime: The Arkansas Prison Scandal* (1970) and *The Dilemma of Prison Reform* (1982). Hollywood told his story, with various fictional elements, in the film *Brubaker* (1980), starring Robert Redford. Murton died in Oklahoma City, at a veteran's hospital, on October 10, 1990.

later a textile mill was built inside the prison, using convict labor to process 500 bales of cotton and 6,000 pounds of wool per year, earning the state an annual $800,000 profit. After the Civil War, Huntsville was the only Confederate prison still standing. It acquired an evil reputation

San Quentin State Prison, located near San Rafael, California, is home to America's largest death row, where all executions in the state are carried out. *AP Photo/Lacy Atkins*

for brutal punishment and exhausting labor through the early 20th century, including participation in the corrupt convict lease system. During the 1930s inmates also ran a large food-canning operation. After World War II renowned penologist Austin MacCormick branded Huntsville "among the worst [prisons] in the United States," prompting reforms under new supervisor Oscar Ellis. Despite those efforts, inmate lawsuits in the 1980s resulted in supervision of Texas prisons by a federal court, which deemed existing regulations unconstitutional.[13]

San Quentin State Prison

San Quentin opened near San Rafael, California, in July 1852, and is the state's oldest lockup. Established as a private prison, San Quentin—or "Q"—reverted to state control after various scandals, including use of a dungeon, sparked public outrage. Today San Quentin occupies 275 acres, including America's largest death row, where all California executions are performed. San Quentin held both male and female inmates until 1932, when California built its first women's prison at Tehachapi. Torture remained "an approved method of interrogation" until 1944, when it was formally banned. A court-ordered report from 2005 found the prison "old, antiquated, dirty, poorly staffed, poorly maintained with inadequate medical space and equipment and overcrowded." Today, despite a yearly operating budget of $210 million, overcrowding remains a problem. Officially designed to hold 3,082 inmates, San Quentin confined more than 5,200 in December 2008, supervised by a staff of 1,718. A new trauma center opened at the prison in 2007, and planning for a $175 million medical complex is ongoing.[14]

5

Federal Prisons

Atlanta, Georgia

In April 1980 the Cuban government announced that any citizens who wished to leave the island for America were free to go. Thousands flocked to the port of Mariel, fleeing Cuba on boats of all kinds, making their way across 90 miles of ocean to Florida. By October, when the so-called Mariel Boatlift ended, some 125,000 Cubans had entered the United States. Of those, 2,746 were identified as prison inmates or mental patients, unacceptable to U.S. Immigration authorities. They were sent to federal prisons in Atlanta and Oakdale, Louisiana, while negotiations for their return to Cuba dragged on for seven years.[1]

Finally, in November 1987, the U.S. State Department announced Cuba's agreement to accept the undesirables. Three days later, on November 13, Cuban inmates seized control of the U.S. Penitentiary in Atlanta, capturing 100 hostages and burning down part of the prison. Another riot erupted at Oakdale on November 21, where Cuban inmates took 28 hostages and burned four buildings. Members of the FBI's Hostage Rescue Team and advisers from the U.S. Army Special Forces (Green Berets) responded to both riot zones, preventing any escapes and negotiating an end to the violence on December 4. Despite the violence, only one person died in the riots: a Cuban inmate shot by an Atlanta guard in self-defense.[2]

Investigation of the riots disclosed problems within the affected prisons. Both were overcrowded. Atlanta's inmate population exceeded its design limit by 47 percent; Oakdale was 81 percent beyond capacity. And authorities at both lockups had rejected suggestions for extra security measures, despite warnings from guards that Cuban inmates might rebel. Despite those findings, Federal Bureau of Prisons Director J. Michael Quinlan told the *New York Times*, "In my own judgment, I don't think [the riots] could have been avoided." Oakdale Warden J. R. Johnson told reporters, "I assumed that [Cuban inmates] would not be happy with the news" of their return to Cuba, granting that "there was a definite problem in the late notification." Atlanta Warden Joseph Petrovsky added, "I guess we weren't prepared."[3]

THE FEDS

America's federal courts and prisons deal with violators of laws passed by Congress, which govern the nation as a whole or specific areas controlled exclusively by the federal government (such as national parks, military bases, Indian reservations, and federal buildings). Those laws are so diverse that simply listing them by name would fill a book. In broad terms, defendants may be tried and punished for federal *regulatory violations* (rules pertaining to government or business operations), misdemeanors, or felonies including capital offenses (including various classes of murder, espionage, and treason).

Dozens of law enforcement agencies pursue federal offenders nationwide. Some of the more famous ones include the FBI; the U.S. Secret Service; the Bureau of Alcohol, Tobacco, Firearms, and Explosives; the Drug Enforcement Administration; the U.S. Marshals Service; U.S. Immigration and Customs Enforcement; and the Internal Revenue Service Criminal Investigations Division. Others, seldom mentioned in the media and little known to most Americans, include the Bureau of Indian Affairs Police, the U.S. Park Police, the Bureau of Engraving and Printing Police, the Veterans Affairs Police, the Smithsonian Institution's National Zoological Park Police, the Tennessee Valley Authority Police, and the Library of Congress Police. In short, "the feds" have an agency for every occasion and offense.

It was not always so. Before 1910 federal agents limited their scrutiny to counterfeiters, tax dodgers, and persons who robbed or defrauded the U.S. government. In 1910 fear of "white slavery"—abduction of females into forced prostitution—prompted passage of the Mann Act, which punished transportation of women across state lines for "immoral purposes." In 1919 the Dyer Act banned driving stolen cars across state lines, and there things rested until 1932, when the Lindbergh kidnapping panicked America and Congress, making interstate abductions a federal offense.[4]

Still, most crimes fell under state jurisdiction, permitting bandits like John Dillinger to rob a bank in one state and flee to another, where police were free to ignore him. It took the Kansas City Massacre—a gangland slaying of five lawmen, including two FBI agents, in June 1933—to spark a federal "war on crime" and prompt passage of new

BATTLE OF ALCATRAZ

Alcatraz Island—"The Rock," in San Francisco Bay—was billed from 1936 to 1963 as America's escape-proof prison. Three prisoners tunneled out of their cells and fled on homemade rafts in June 1962, but while their disappearance later inspired a film starring Clint Eastwood (*Escape from Alcatraz,* 1979), prison authorities still insist that the three inmates drowned and were swept out to sea by the tides.

A very different, more violent escape attempt was launched by six convicts in May 1946, igniting a conflict known as the "Battle of Alcatraz." Inmate participants included Bernard Coy, a bank robber serving 26 years; Joseph Cretzer, serving life for murder; Arnold Kyle, Cretzer's brother-in-law, serving life for bank robbery, murder, and assault; Sam Shockley, doing life for bank robbery and kidnapping; and Floyd Barkdoll, another bank robber. Coy was the "brains" of the gang, spending months in advance observing the movements of Alcatraz guards.

After lunch on May 2, Coy smeared himself with axle grease and pried apart the bars of his cell, wriggling out to reach the prison's West End Gun Gallery. There, he clubbed a guard unconscious, seized weapons, and freed his five accomplices. Two more would-be escapees, Miriam Thompson (serving 99 laws expanding federal authority. Those statutes, passed in 1934, punished robbery of banks that carried federal insurance, assaults on federal agents, possession of "gangster weapons" such as machine guns, and interstate flight to avoid trial or imprisonment. Over the years since 1934, federal jurisdiction has grown to the point where some Americans complain that Washington runs every aspect of our lives, from cradle to grave.

FEDERAL PRISONS

Federal lockups have existed from the earliest days of the United States, beginning with converted colonial jails. As the nation expanded

years for a kidnap-murder) and Clarence Carnes (another killer and The Rock's youngest inmate at age 19) also joined the breakout crew. The inmates soon captured nine unarmed guards and locked them in cells, but not before one officer hid the key that would free them into the exercise yard.

Their plan dissolved from there, as sirens wailed, guards rallied, and U.S. Marines mobilized to support prison officers. When the battle smoke cleared, five men were dead, including officers William Miller and Harold Stites, with inmates Coy, Cretzer, and Marvin Hubbard, a kidnapper transferred to Alcatraz after a 1944 riot at the Atlanta federal lockup. Thirteen other guards and one inmate were wounded by gunfire during the firefight.[5]

Rioters Shockley and Thompson were charged with murder after the Battle of Alcatraz. Jurors convicted both inmates, and they were executed together in San Quentin's gas chamber on December 3, 1948. Clarence Carnes received another 99-year sentence for his role in the battle, boosting his federal time to a total of 203 years. He remained at Alcatraz until it closed in 1963, and then spent another 10 years at Leavenworth before he was paroled, at age 46. Parole violations soon returned Carnes to prison, however, and AIDS claimed his life in October 1988, at Springfield, Missouri's Medical Center for Federal Prisoners.

westward, territorial prisons were built to house inmates from regions awaiting transition to statehood. A case in point is McNeil Island, Washington, created as a territorial prison in 1875, formally transferred to control by the U.S. Department of Justice in 1904.

In 1891 Congress passed the Three Prisons Act, authorizing creation of federal prisons at Leavenworth, Kansas (operated as a military prison since 1875), Atlanta, and McNeil Island. Those prisons began receiving inmates under new management in 1897, 1902, and 1904, respectively. Responsibility for supervising federal prisons passed to a general agent of the Justice Department in 1907, and remained in his hands until Congress created the Federal Bureau of Prisons (FBP) in 1930.

By that time there were 11 federal prisons nationwide. Today, the FBP network includes 115 prisons, 28 community corrections offices, six regional offices, two staff training centers, and a central administrative office. As of June 30, 2008, the federal prison system confined 201,142 inmates. Eighty-two percent of those were housed in federal lockups, while 12 percent were held in privately run facilities or local jails.[6]

Beyond those basic facts, reported by the FBP itself, information on life inside federal prisons remains limited. It is known that 24 federal prison guards lost their lives on duty between November 1901 and June 2008, and that the federal government has executed 37 civilian inmates since August 1927, but much remains unknown.[7] The Death in Custody Reporting Act of 2000 applies only to state and local institutions, leaving inmate deaths in federal lockups unreported to the public or to Congress. Meanwhile, reports on racial composition of American inmate populations, compiled by the Bureau of Justice Statistics, combine totals from state and federal institutions, without a specific breakdown.[8]

MILITARY PRISONS

Officers and enlisted members of the American armed forces were governed by Articles of War from June 1775 to May 1951, when a new Uniform Code of Military Justice (UCMJ) replaced former regulations. Offenses punished under the UCMJ include normal crimes such as theft, robbery, rape, and murder, plus violations of rules that have no application to civilians. Examples include mutiny, desertion, being absent without official leave (AWOL), refusal to obey lawful orders, and insubordination toward superior officers.

Each branch of the U.S. military has its own police force. Members of the army answer to the Military Police Corps, while air force personnel are supervised by the Air Force Office of Special Investigations, and members of the U.S. Navy and Marine Corps are controlled by the Naval Criminal Investigative Service. Military defendants are tried by courts-martial (military or naval courts), with members of the court appointed by a commanding officer. Punishment, upon conviction, may range from reduction in rank to a less-than-honorable discharge from service, imprisonment, or execution in the case of capital offenses.

As with investigative agencies, each military branch maintains its own prisons and detention facilities. The only maximum security prison run by the Department of Defense is the U.S. Disciplinary Barracks at Fort Leavenworth, Kansas, remodeled as a state-of-the-art facility in 2002. Operating under the motto "Our Mission, Your Future," Fort Leavenworth houses military defendants serving long-term sentences. Inmate programs offer "individual treatment to inmates to prepare them for a self-reliant, trustworthy and respectable future . . . emphasizing behavior, education, vocational skills and a chance to choose."[9]

Aside from Fort Leavenworth, the U.S. Army has six regional confinement facilities at Fort Carson, Colorado; Fort Knox, Kentucky; Fort Lewis, Washington; Fort Sill, Oklahoma; the U.S. Army Garrison in Mannheim, Germany; and at Camp Humphreys, South Korea. Air Force confinement facilities are found at Kirtland Air Force Base in New Mexico, and at Lackland Air Force Base in Texas. The U.S. Navy calls its prisons "brigs." At last count, 24 existed on land, found at Navy and Marine Corps bases across the United States and around the world, in Puerto Rico, Spain, Italy, Iceland, Japan, Guam, and on the island of Diego Garcia in the Indian Ocean. Naval pre-trial confinement facilities are found in Connecticut, Illinois, Japan, and at Guantanamo Bay, Cuba. At the time of this writing, at least 23 naval ships also had brigs of their own to deal with offenses committed at sea.[10]

Under the UCMJ, military personnel may be sentenced to death for 14 offenses, including murder, rape, espionage, mutiny or sedition,

(continues on page 64)

ADX FLORENCE

The U.S. Penitentiary Administrative Maximum Facility in Florence, Colorado, is a federal supermax prison, commonly known as ADX Florence or "the Alcatraz of the Rockies."[11] It houses prisoners who are ranked as the most dangerous FBP inmates, demanding the tightest control.

ADX Florence was built in response to an incident at the federal prison in Marion, Illinois, where two guards were killed by inmates in October 1983. That double murder transformed Marion into a "control unit" prison, but FBP Director Norman Carlson persuaded Congress to approve construction of another, more modern supermax facility in Colorado, built on 37 acres at a cost exceeding $60 million. ADX Florence received its first inmates in November 1994. Today, Guinness World Records ranks it as the world's most secure prison, equipped with 1,400 remote-controlled steel doors, barbed-wire fences, attack dogs, and other security

Guard towers loom over the administrative maximum security facility, the highest security area at the Federal Prison in Florence, Colorado. The prison, commonly referred to as ADX Florence, holds prisoners considered to be the most dangerous in the country. *AP Photo/Pueblo Chieftain, Chris McLean*

devices, including laser beams and pressure pads to warn of unauthorized movement.[12]

Inmates at ADX Florence spend 23 hours per day in their soundproof cells, measuring 84 square feet. The "free" hour permits them to exercise, while handcuffed and shackled, in a somewhat larger concrete cell. As former FBP official James Aitken told *The Times* of London in 2006, "They are in a security envelope, a security bubble. Their environment is sterile, they are isolated from the outside world and from the prison world."[13]

According to FBP statistics, ADX Florence held 475 prisoners in 2007, with 15 cells vacant. Ninety-seven percent of its inmates had been transferred from other prisons, 22 percent had killed fellow inmates, and 35 percent had attacked other inmates or guards. Inmates recently confined to ADX Florence include 39 convicted terrorists, 15 members of street or prison gangs, and 16 members of the Mafia or other organized crime groups.[14] Individual notorious inmates have included

- Charles Harrelson, father of actor Woody Harrelson and a contract killer, convicted of murdering a federal judge in 1979, killed by a heart attack in 2007
- Antonio Guerrero Rodriguez, a Cuban spy serving life plus 10 years
- Matthew Hale, a neo-Nazi cult leader sentenced for plotting to murder a federal judge
- "Unabomber" Theodore Kaczynzki, sentenced to life for three murders
- Dr. Michael Swango, a serial-killing physician with victims in the United States and Africa
- Robert Hanssen, a former FBI agent sentenced to life for selling American secrets to Russia
- Eric Rudolph, a "pro-life" extremist convicted of bombings that killed three persons and wounded more than 100 in 1996–1997
- Hubert "Rap" Brown, a 1960s radical and convicted robber, sentenced to life for killing a Georgia policeman in March 2000, transferred to ADX Florence in 2007 when state prison guards found him unmanageable

(continued from page 61)

aiding the enemy, "forcing a safeguard," misusing a countersign, a "subordinate compelling surrender," and so on. During wartime, personnel may also be executed for desertion, assaulting or disobeying superior

A cell inside the U.S. Disciplinary Barracks at Fort Leavenworth is unoccupied. The prison, run by the Department of Defense, is for military offenders serving lengthy sentences. *AP Photo/U.S. Army*

officers, and for "misbehavior of a sentinel or lookout." While no military execution statistics exist for the full span of U.S. history, or for all service branches, it is known that the U.S. Army has executed 135 soldiers since 1916, and that 160 members of all services were executed between 1942 and 1961. The U.S. Navy has performed no executions since 1849, and no military executions have occurred since 1961. Fifteen defendants have received death sentences since 1984, but six of those had their sentences revised on appeal, leaving nine on death row at the time of this writing.[15]

"INDIAN COUNTRY"

The federal government owns three kinds of land in the United States: public, military, and Indian. Nationwide, 326 reservations and other specific regions—56.2 million acres in all—are set aside for Native Americans, collectively described in federal publications as "Indian Country."[16]

In 2002 the federal government published a *Census of Tribal Justice Agencies in American Indian Jurisdictions*, based on information collected from 314 tribes nationwide. According to that report, aside from Bureau of Indian Affairs Police, 165 tribes maintained their own law enforcement agencies, 188 conducted trials of criminal defendants, and 71 operated detention facilities. Another survey, in 2007, found 83 jails in Indian Country, holding 2,163 inmates (up from 1,745 held in 68 tribal jails during 2004). Forty percent of those jailed in 2007 were held for violent crimes. Of those, 20 percent were convicted of domestic violence, 13 percent for simple or aggravated assault, 2 percent for rape or sexual assault, and 6 percent for other unspecified offenses. On average, jails in Indian Country received 158 new prisoners per month.[17]

DEATH ROW

Federal executions are supervised by members of the U.S. Marshals Service. The first such execution on record occurred on June 25, 1790, when Thomas Bird was hanged in Maine by U.S. Marshal Henry Dearborn, for murder on the high seas.[18] Files maintained over the next 137 years make no distinction between state and federal executions, and the only tally kept by the federal government begins in August 1927, with murder defendant James Aldermon's hanging in Florida. Over the next 76 years, 36 more federal inmates were put to death on charges including murder (19), kidnapping (6), sabotage (6), espionage (2), rape (2), and bank robbery (1).[19]

At the time of this writing, 57 federal inmates were held under sentence of death for crimes committed in 26 different states. Their crimes included offenses committed under the Omnibus Anti-Drug Abuse Act of 1988 (permitting execution for murders related to drug-trafficking) and the Federal Death Penalty Act of 1994 (allowing execution for 60 offenses, including homicides, espionage or treason, and various non-homicidal narcotics offenses). Of the condemned defendants, 55 were male and two were female; 22 were white, 28 were African American, six were Hispanic, and one was Native American.[20]

6

Capital Punishment

Death Row, U.S.A.

In 1999 *The Green Mile* won 13 film awards and secured another 27 nominations, including four Academy Awards for Best Picture, Best Actor, Best Writing, and Best Music.[1] It also shocked some viewers with a scene in which a cruel prison guard, portrayed by Doug Hutchinson, sabotages the execution of an inmate he despises, causing the electric chair to malfunction and burst into flames. While that scene was horrific, few who watched it realized that such things also happen in real life.

No reporters witnessed the Virginia execution of Frank Coppola in August 1982, but an attorney present claims that Coppola's scalp and pants caught fire, filling the death chamber with smoke.[2]

In April 1983, John Evans suffered a similar fate in Alabama, flames leaping from his head and leg during a protracted 14-minute electrocution.[3]

Multiple high-voltage shocks were required to kill Georgia convict Alpha Stephens in December 1984, prompting a prison guard to say that "Stephens was just not a conductor" of electricity.[4]

Indiana prison authorities admitted that the October 1985 execution of William Vandiver "did not go according to plan." In fact, five shocks of 2,300 volts each, spanning 17 minutes, were required to do the job.[5]

Alabama inmate Horace Dunkins Jr. suffered a 19-minute execution in June 1989, interrupted when a guard announced, "I believe we've got the jacks on wrong." Prison spokesmen blamed the botched execution on "human error."[6]

Jesse Tafero burst into flames on May 4, 1990, as Florida's electric chair malfunctioned due to "inadvertent human error." Their media re-creation of the event set fire to a household toaster, used as a substitute "inmate."[7]

Six months later, in Virginia, inmate Wilbert Evans hemorrhaged before startled witnesses, as the electric chair elevated his preexisting high blood pressure.[8]

Another Florida inmate, Pedro Medina, caught fire as the electric chair—dubbed "Old Sparky"—malfunctioned again in March 1997.[9]

Allen Davis, yet another unfortunate Florida convict, suffered massive hemorrhaging in "Old Sparky" in June 1999. Viewing photos of the execution, Justice Leander Shaw of the state supreme court declared that "for all appearances," Davis "was brutally tortured to death by the citizens of Florida."[10]

CONDEMNED TO DIE

All known societies have executed prisoners at some point in their history. The impulse to kill in retaliation for crime is ancient, dating from the Code of Ur-Nammu (2100–2050 B.C.) and the Code of Hammurabi (1790 B.C.), which prescribed death for murderers, robbers, kidnappers, and persons who falsely accused others of criminal activity. The Old Testament extended capital punishment from killers and kidnappers to adulterers, false prophets, witches and sorcerers, homosexuals, rebellious children, Sabbath violators, and anyone engaged in premarital sex.[11]

England's monarchy waffled on capital punishment. William the Conqueror, king from 1066 to 1087 A.D., permitted executions only during wartime, while Henry VIII executed 72,000 prisoners between 1509 and 1547. By the early 1700s execution was prescribed for 222 different offenses, including theft and poaching deer or rabbits on royal land. During the 20th century, half of those crimes were stricken from the list, but many capital offenses remained.[12]

Florida's electric chair, nicknamed "Old Sparky," has a history of malfunctioning during executions. *AP Photo/Mark Foley*

Early American colonists typically followed the laws of their native countries, including punishment of capital crimes. Present-day America's first known execution occurred in 1608, when George Kendall was shot for spying in Virginia. Before the outbreak of the Revolutionary War, 167 years later, at least 938 colonists were executed for various offenses. Their crimes included murder (302), piracy (103), burglary (99), slave rebellions (75), theft (59), sexual offenses (40), witchcraft (35), arson (17), counterfeiting (16), and treason (10). In 111 cases no specific charge was recorded, but all felonies rated punishment by death in the 18th century.[13]

OPERATION ABOLITION

Some Americans have always opposed capital punishment, beginning with early Quakers who condemned all forms of violence. Four Quakers were executed by Massachusetts Puritans during 1659–1660, for their religious beliefs, which increased the sect's opposition to the death penalty. Before the Revolutionary War, Thomas Jefferson proposed a law that would limit Virginia executions to murderers and traitors, but colonial lawmakers defeated the measure by a single vote.[14]

Pennsylvania was the first state to restrict capital punishment, in 1794, when lawmakers limited execution to defendants convicted of *first-degree* (premeditated) murder. A half-century later, in 1846, Michigan eliminated capital punishment for all crimes except treason. Other states initiated *discretionary sentencing,* allowing judges to choose between death or prison terms for many felonies. The abolition movement faltered with invention of the more "humane" electric chair—first used to execute New York inmate William Kemmler in August 1890—but six states banned all executions between 1907 and 1917, while three more limited death sentences to traitors and those who killed police officers.[15]

Those reforms were barely in place when the "Red Scare" of 1919–1920 prompted five of the six abolitionist states to restore capital punishment. Reformers took another hit in 1924, with introduction of "humane" lethal gas chambers, first used to execute Nevada inmate Gee Jon in February 1924. Throughout the Roaring Twenties and the Great Depression, executions escalated to an average rate of 167 per year during the 1930s.[16]

LYNCH LAW

Lynching is the mob execution of one or more victims, often—but not always—accused of some crime or social offense. One person cannot lynch another; by law, it requires at least two killers. Many historians believe that lynching got its name from Virginia planter Charles Lynch (1736-1796), who led an unofficial "court" to punish British loyalists during the Revolutionary War.[17]

Most early lynchings occurred in regions where official law enforcement was absent or ineffective. Between 1767 and 1900, residents of 32 states formed at least 326 "vigilance committees"—source of the term *vigilante*—to privately enforce various laws. Those groups lynched at least 735 persons, though records are far from complete.[18]

After the Civil War, random mobs and racist groups like the Ku Klux Klan changed the nature of American lynching. While many victims were still accused of crimes, often falsely, nonwhites also suffered attacks for "offenses" such as "insulting" whites, refusing to sell their property on demand—and, in one case, for "frightening a white man's cow." No reliable statistics for modern lynchings exist before 1882, when Alabama's Tuskegee Institute began keeping detailed records. According to those files, 3,437 African Americans and 1,293 whites were lynched between 1882 and 1968. Other sources claim higher totals, including one Web site listing 6,000 African Americans lynched between 1865 and 1965.[19]

From 1922 onward, Congress debated several antilynching bills, but all were blocked by southern senators. FBI Director J. Edgar Hoover (1895–1972) also opposed antilynching legislation as a violation of "states rights." The last recognized American lynching occurred in June 1998, when three white Texans affiliated with the Ku Klux Klan kidnapped black victim James Byrd Jr. and dragged him behind a pickup truck to his death. Two of the lynchers were sentenced to die, while the third received a life prison term.

The horrors of World War II, climaxed by trial and execution of nearly 1,100 German and Japanese war criminals, swung public sentiment against capital punishment. Executions declined nationwide, from 1,289 in the 1940s to 715 in the 1950s, while only 191 inmates were executed in the 1960s, for an official total of 14,489 put to death since 1608.[20]

THE "CLASS OF '72"

In the 1960s, the U.S. Supreme Court began "fine tuning" the practice of capital punishment. Two cases from 1968—*U.S. v. Jackson* and *Witherspoon v. Illinois*—limited federal executions for kidnapping and banned state prosecutors from restricting jury membership to supporters of execution. Four years later, in *Furman v. Georgia* and two related cases, the court banned "arbitrary and capricious" sentences of death for crimes that resulted in no loss of life. That ruling affected 40 states, where 629 condemned inmates—later dubbed "the Class of '72"—found their sentences commuted to life imprisonment.[21]

Furman v. Georgia did not ban all executions, only those deemed "excessive" or those where verdicts were affected by a defendant's race, social status, or other irrelevant factors. Thirty-four states passed new capital punishment statutes, outlining various "special circumstances" which, combined with murder, made a killer eligible for death row. During 1976 the Supreme Court approved those efforts in a series of cases, including *Woodson v. North Carolina, Gregg v. Georgia, Jurek v. Texas*, and *Proffitt v. Florida*.[22]

The first defendant executed under those new guidelines, Gary Gilmore, was shot by a Utah firing squad in January 1977. Between that date and June 2009, another 1,167 inmates were executed, while 3,220 remain under sentence of death in 36 states that still practice capital punishment. Of those states, one—New Hampshire—has performed no executions since 1939 and has no inmates presently condemned.[23]

PROS AND CONS

Modern supporters of execution defend capital punishment on moral, economic, and practical grounds. Some say that executions should continue because they are "God's will," decreed in the Bible. Most claim

"TOOKIE" WILLIAMS

Stanley "Tookie" Williams III (1953–2005) was born in New Orleans and moved to Los Angeles with his family, as a child. There, at age 18, he helped organize a youth group called the "Cribs," later known as the "Crips." While Williams described the original gang as a kind of Neighborhood Watch group, it soon turned to crime, trafficking in crack cocaine and waging bloody war against a rival gang, the Bloods.

On February 28, 1979, Williams and two other Crips robbed a convenience store in Whittier, California, where Williams shot and killed clerk Albert Owens. On March 11 Williams alone invaded a motel in South Central L.A., killing the owner, his wife, and son, before fleeing with $120 from the cash register. Convicted on four counts of first-degree murder and two counts of robbery, Williams received a death sentence in April 1981.

Williams was far from a model prisoner on death row. Over the next 12 years he was involved in multiple attacks on guards and other inmates, as well as several failed escape attempts, spending six and a half years in solitary confinement. Then, after a shower brawl in 1993, he seemed to undergo a change, campaigning against violent gangs, posting an Internet apology for his role in creating the Crips, and writing a memoir—*Blue Rage, Black Redemption*—that was published in 2004. That same year, he tried to negotiate a truce between the Crips and Bloods, prompting President George W. Bush to grant him a "Call to Service Award."

But nothing helped Williams with his legal appeals. Friends in the free world, including ministers, celebrities, and Nobel Prize-winners joined in calls for commutation of his sentence, while spokesmen for the Los Angeles Police Department, L.A.'s district attorney, and other officials challenged his reformation. Some say Williams hurt his own case by refusing to "snitch" on other Crips suspected of violent crimes. California's Supreme Court rejected his last appeal on November 30, 2005, and Governor Arnold Schwarzenegger denied a plea for clemency on December 12. The following day, Williams was executed by lethal injection at San Quentin.

that execution of convicted killers is cheaper than keeping them locked up for life, therefore a benefit to taxpayers. Many also defend execution as a deterrent to future murders by other felons, and as the only guarantee that imprisoned killers will not escape or be paroled to claim more victims.

Opponents of capital punishment counter those assertions with the following arguments:

- Aside from murder, no other biblical crimes rate execution today, thus making religious arguments invalid.
- Capital punishment, including mandatory appeals and reviews, actually costs *more* than jailing killers for life. According to various reports (which supporters of execution dismiss as inaccurate), California spends an average of $250 million per execution, Florida spends $24 million to kill one inmate, and Texas spends $2.3 million per capital case—three times the cost of housing and feeding a convict in maximum security for 40 years.[24]
- Third-party deterrence was rejected by 84 percent of professional criminologists polled nationwide in 1984. Support for that view comes from 16 southern states, which have performed 82.4 percent of all American executions since 1977. In 2007, according to the FBI, those same states suffered nearly half (46 percent) of all murders committed nationwide. If executions deter crime, critics ask, why is the South the most dangerous region in the United States, with seven murders and 549 violent crimes per 100,000 residents?[25]

Other common arguments against capital punishment include racial bias and the danger of wrongful convictions. Statistics show that the number of African Americans imprisoned far exceeds their percentage of the U.S. population, and capital punishment strikes equally hard at minorities. Of the inmates executed since 1977, 55.9 percent were white, 34.7 percent were African American, 7.4 percent were Hispanic, and 2 percent were "others." Among the inmates still on death row nationwide, 45 percent are white, 42 percent are African American, 11 percent are Hispanic, and 2 percent are "others."[26]

Greater inequity emerges if interracial murders are examined. Each year, approximately half of all American murder victims are white.

Police "cleared" 61.2 percent of all murders in 2007, arresting 13,480 suspects. Of those, 47.6 percent were white, 50.4 percent were African American, and 2 percent were "others." However, when it came to inter-racial homicides, only 15 white defendants were executed for killing black victims between 1977 and 2009, while 242 African Americans were executed for killing whites.[27]

Critics claim that those statistics prove a deadly bias against minority defendants charged with slaying white victims, while white killers of blacks are normally allowed to live. Supporters of capital punishment reply that nonwhites commit more murders than white felons do—a claim not supported by FBI statistics.

Few issues trouble both sides more than the question of innocent persons sentenced to die. Since 1989 at least 192 American prison inmates—including 14 on death row—have been exonerated and released due to DNA testing of evidence linked to their alleged crimes. Other forms of evidence freed an additional 119 innocent death row inmates in 26 states, between 1973 and 2008. Most of those wrongful convictions were based on mistaken eyewitness testimony, but fear of official misconduct—"frame-ups"—also persists. In 2000, following revelations that Cook County police and prosecutors had suppressed and falsified evidence in capital cases, Governor George Ryan commuted all Illinois death sentences and imposed a moratorium on executions that continues to this day.[28]

Despite that move in one state, and continued challenges in other cases by groups like the Innocence Project, opponents of capital punishment still fear that innocent defendants have been executed in the past and will be again, in the future, as long as executions continue.

EXECUTING JUVENILES

Another heated issue concerns capital punishment of juvenile offenders. Before 1908, felons of any age risked execution in Britain. The youngest ever hanged was eight-year-old arsonist John Dean, in 1629. An 11-year-old girl, Alicia Glaston, was hanged for unspecified crimes in 1546.[29]

American records of capital punishment rarely list defendants' ages before the 19th century, and ages were not consistently recorded until the 1940s. Still, we know that colonial Massachusetts and Pennsylvania executed two 16-year-old boys and three 17-year-olds. Four of the five defendants were white. Three were hanged for murder, and two for sodomy (both in Puritan Massachusetts).[30]

Between the Revolutionary War and Civil War, 13 states executed a total of 21 juveniles. Two of the 13 were girls. Three were 12 years old, two were 13, one was 14, six were 16, and nine were 17. Their crimes included murder (13), arson (4), attempted murder (1), attempted rape (1), espionage (1), and "other" (1).[31]

From Reconstruction through the end of the 19th century, 18 states executed 39 juveniles. The youngest was 13, two were 14, three were 15, 11 were 16, and 22 were 17. Eighty-seven percent were executed in southern states, which may explain why 22 were African American. The rest included 12 whites, two Native Americans, one Hispanic, one Asian American, and one of unknown race. Their crimes included 33 murders and six rapes.[32]

Between 1900 and 1959, the last year with a juvenile execution in America, 20 states executed 80 minors. The youngest was 14, while three were 15, 13 were 16, and 63 were 17 years old. All but 10 executions of minors occurred in the South. Sixty-six of those executed were African American, 11 were white, and three were Hispanic. Their crimes included murder (58), rape (20), attempted rape (1), and robbery (1).[33]

No juvenile inmates have been executed in America since 1977, but 22 persons convicted of murders committed at age 17 were executed between 1977 and 2003. All were in their 20s or older when put to death, because legal appeals had postponed their executions.[34]

In the case of *Thompson v. Oklahoma* (1988), five Supreme Court justices ruled that execution of killers convicted below age 16 is unconstitutional. A year later, in *Stanford v. Kentucky* and *Wilkins v. Missouri,* the court approved execution of defendants aged 16 and 17. Nineteen states presently ban execution of anyone convicted below age 18, a rule confirmed by the Supreme Court in *Roper v. Simmons* (2005). That decision commuted the death sentences of 29 Texas inmates and 14 in Alabama.[35]

Alternative Sentencing

Los Angeles, California

Celebrities are special. Fame and fortune sets them apart in every aspect of life. While millions of Americans adore actors, musicians, models, and other public figures, some complain that celebrities have it too easy in court—and in jail.

September 2006: Hotel heiress and actress Paris Hilton was arrested in L.A. for driving while intoxicated. She dismissed the arrest as "nothing," but the courts took a different view after Hilton was stopped twice more, for driving with a suspended license. Sentenced to a month in county jail, she served 23 days in June 2007, and then emerged to protest her "raw deal" on CNN's *Larry King Live*.[1]

March 2007: Television personality Khloe Kardashian was arrested for drunk driving. She received three years' probation but failed to complete her community service or to attend court-ordered alcohol education classes. Slapped with a 30-day jail sentence in July 2008, Kardashian spent only one hour and 13 minutes in custody.[2]

May 2007: Actress Lindsay Lohan crashed her car into a roadside tree. Police found cocaine in the Mercedes-Benz and arrested Lohan for possession. Two months later, after a high-speed chase with media photographers, officers found more drugs in her car. In August 2007 she received a four-day jail sentence, which was immediately cut in half with credit for time already served. In fact, Lohan spent only 84 minutes in custody when she reported to jail on November 16.[3]

February 2009: Actor-musician Chris Brown assaulted his girl-friend, pop singer Rhianna, leaving her bloody and bruised. Four months later, Brown negotiated a plea bargain that spared him from prison. Instead, the court imposed five years' probation, with six months of community service. Brown was ordered to stay at least 50 yards away from Rhianna, except during Hollywood events, when the distance was reduced to 30 feet.[4]

AVOIDING JAIL

Except in cases where state or federal law demands a prison sentence, courts are free to explore alternative sentencing. Some alternative sentences relieve defendants of any jail or prison time, while others may reduce the time served. Some judges use alternative sentencing to relieve overcrowding of jails and prisons, while others seek creative ways to reform offenders.

Financial penalties are frequently imposed as an alternative to—or in addition to—incarceration. Fines are payments made directly to the court or government, varying from small amounts in the case of local offenses to millions of dollars for serious felons. Restitution involves court-ordered payments made directly to an offender's victims, in compensation for medical bills and lost or damaged property. Convicted defendants are sometimes required to pay court costs, in effect financing their own prosecutions. Various laws also permit seizure and forfeiture of cash and other property obtained through criminal activity, usually in cases involving drugs and organized crime.

Another common form of alternative sentencing is probation (from the Latin *probatio*, meaning "testing"), which—like financial penalties—may be imposed with or without prison time. Many jurisdictions define "probational" offenses, while demanding incarceration for other crimes. All forms of probation require that defendants abstain from any illegal behavior, but otherwise they vary widely from case to case. Violation of any court-imposed rules may, as in the Kardashian case described above, result in confinement. Common terms of probation include:

- Psychiatric counseling or other forms of remedial activity, including driver-education courses, anger-management classes, education in the undesirable effects of alcohol and drugs, and so on.

- Orders forbidding contact between the defendant and his or her victims or known criminal associates.
- Avoidance of any organizations that may have provoked or influenced an offender's criminal conduct, including gangs, political or religious extremist groups, and so on.
- Limitations on a defendant's travel within or outside of a court's jurisdiction, including surrender of one's passports if authorities fear an offender may flee the country.
- A ban on possession or firearms or other weapons, particularly in the case of violent offenders.
- A ban on various activities related to the offender's crimes, including possession of animals (in cruelty cases) or computers (for convicted hackers), driving motor vehicles (for drunk or reckless drivers), or even use of telephones except in dire emergencies (in cases of telephone fraud or harassment).
- Court-ordered community service, frequently tailored to suit a defendant's crime. Thus, celebrity drunk-drivers may be required to film public service announcements warning other motorists, or vandals might be required to paint over graffiti, and so on.

Probation may be either supervised or unsupervised. Supervised probation may be intensive or standard. Intensive supervision commonly includes house arrest, electronic or satellite tracking devices, periodic tests for alcohol or drugs, unannounced home or workplace visits, and waiver of a defendant's Fourth Amendment freedom from searches without legal warrants. Under standard supervision, defendants normally report to a probation officer at scheduled intervals, while completing any court-ordered counseling, classes, or community service assignments. Unsupervised probation requires no oversight, but any arrests occurring during the term of probation may return the defendant to custody. In December 2007 a total of 4,293,163 adult Americans were serving various terms of probation.[5]

Jail or prison terms are often suspended at a judge's discretion, in cases where the law requires no mandatory period of incarceration. The court may suspend all or part of a prison term—for example, requiring an offender to serve six months of a two-year sentence, with 18 months suspended. Suspended sentences are equivalent to probation, with any further violations during the suspended portion commonly requiring an offender to serve his full sentence in custody. Sentences are normally suspended as part of a plea bargain, often to reward defendants who return stolen property, testify against criminal accomplices, and so on.

HOUSE ARREST

House arrest—also called home confinement, home detention, or electronic monitoring—limits an offender's movements to varying degrees. In juvenile cases, offenders are generally permitted to attend school, and sometimes hold a job, but otherwise are not allowed to leave their homes. Adult offenders, likewise, may be permitted to work, buy groceries, or perform community service, while outside recreational activities are banned.

The terms of house arrest also frequently limit or ban electronic communication with persons outside an offender's immediate family, including use of telephones, computers, and other devices. If electronic communications are permitted by the court, they may be monitored by probation officers to intercept and punish any illegal or abusive communications.

Defendants sentenced to house arrest are supervised in various ways. Home visits by probation officers, often unannounced, catch straying offenders and may include searches for contraband items. Electronic sensors, commonly locked on a defendant's ankle, allow probation officers to track an offender's movements and may trigger alarms if the subject leaves his home or yard. Most sensors also signal any attempt to remove or deactivate the device. Addition of a GPS (global positioning satellite) device allows police to locate offenders who flee their homes, regardless of how fast and how far they travel.

CORPORAL PUNISHMENT

Corporal punishment involves the infliction of physical pain, commonly by means of whipping (also known as flogging). The British army and navy flogged enlisted men for various offenses, including the case of Private Frederick White—who died during an 1847 whipping at a cavalry barracks in Hounslow, England. Naval floggings sometimes prompted British sailors to rebel, as in the mutiny aboard HMS *Bounty* in 1789.

A juvenile probation officer displays a GPS device, which is commonly used to track offenders sentenced to house arrest. *AP Photo/Suchat Pederson*

In the United States both slaves and criminal defendants suffered whippings from colonial times into the 20th century. The practice lingered longest in Dixie, where Arkansas lawmakers permitted prison floggings until 1968, and some notorious cases made global headlines. Police in Leon County, Florida, arrested Martin Tabert for vagrancy in 1921. Ordered to pay a $25 fine or spend three months at hard labor, Tabert entered the state's convict lease system, where the owners of a lumber company whipped him to death in February 1922. That case prompted Governor Cary Hardee to ban both prison whippings and convict leases, though the corrupt system was not finally eradicated until 1923.[6]

Elsewhere, during Prohibition and the Great Depression, fear of "crime waves" prompted several states to legalize whipping. Delaware led the pack in 1921, imposing 40 lashes on convicted robbers, *plus* 20 years in prison and a $500 fine. Michigan legalized whipping of bank robbers in 1927, while two years later, Indianapolis authorities prescribed flogging for persons convicted of carrying firearms. In 1931 Oklahoma Governor William Murray announced that whipping had reduced his state's crime rate. North Carolina resumed flogging for petty offenses, to relieve jail overcrowding, in 1933. New York and Pennsylvania considered resumption of whipping, but never followed through. Meanwhile, in 1926, an Alabama prison warden faced murder charges for fatal dunkings of inmates in hot and cold water.[7]

Today, only children are subject to corporal punishment in America. Twenty-two states nationwide allow some form of paddling or spanking in public schools, administered by principals or teachers under guidelines established by law. All 50 states permit corporal punishment at home, despite ongoing debates and failed attempts to ban it by law in California and Massachusetts.[8]

SHAMING

Early American colonists often used shaming—public humiliation—as an alternative to prison. Nonviolent offenders might be forced to wear a sign or symbol of their "crime"— such as a letter *A* for adultery—or be held outdoors in the pillory or stocks, subjected to taunts and volleys of rotten fruit from their neighbors. Such penalties fell out of favor after the Revolutionary War, but enjoyed a new vogue in the late 20th century.

Since the 1980s local judges have used shaming as punishment for various offenses. After an elderly Illinois man beat one of his neighbors with a metal pipe, he was sentenced to keep a sign on his lawn for 30 months, reading "A Violent Felon Lives Here. Travel at Your Own Risk." Similar cases emerged from Florida and Oregon, but when a New York judge ordered special license plates for drunk drivers, an appellate court declared the move illegal. Likewise, the Tennessee Supreme Court blocked orders for a convicted child molester to place warning signs outside his home. The courts of Texas disagreed, enforcing a judge's order that 69-year-old Russell Teeter wear a T-shirt reading "I am a registered sex offender" for 22 months, after completing a 60-day jail term.[9]

A variation on shaming—described by proponents as a public safety measure, rather than punishment—involves registration of convicted sex offenders. All states require convicted sex criminals to register with police in their home jurisdiction, and many states now maintain lists

SCARED STRAIGHT

In 1978 director Arnold Shapiro released a documentary film titled *Scared Straight!* Actor Peter Falk narrated the account of a program carried out at New Jersey's Rahway State Prison, where juvenile offenders met adult "lifers," hearing their prison stories and enduring verbal abuse on camera. Aired repeatedly on television in the late 1970s, *Scared Straight!* won an Academy Award for Best Documentary in 1978, prompting sequels that included *Scared Straight! Another Story* (1980), *Scared Straight! 10 Years Later* (1987), and *Scared Straight! 20 Years Later* (1999). The last installment, narrated by actor Danny Glover, reported that 90-plus percent of the young offenders filmed in 1978 still led law-abiding lives.[10]

Several other states launched "scared straight" programs for juvenile offenders in the 1980s, as a result of the TV broadcasts. One penologist who rejected the method was Anthony Schembri, former inspector general for the New York City Department of Correction, later appointed to lead Florida's Department of Juvenile Justice. Schembri described "scared straight" programs as "throwing good money after bad" in a fruitless attempt to cure youthful antisocial behavior through fear. According to Schembri, statistical analysis of various state programs led researchers "to conclude that participating in the Scared Straight program actually correlates with an increase in re-offending compared to a control group of youth who received no intervention at all."[11]

Schembri further declared that "While popular and often declared successful by many practitioners claiming intuitive knowledge of accomplishment and citing testimonials from participants, the empirical status of Scared Straight programs is not nearly as promising. The confrontational style utilized in the original Scared Straight program remains the most popular, yet other programs are designed to be more educational with interactive discussions between the inmates and the youth."[12]

of convicted offenders accessible online, in addition to a National Sex Offender Registry. Supporters of registration say that public identification helps potential victims or their parents avoid sexual predators. Opponents claim that public registration encourages vigilante harassment of defendants who have "paid their debt" in prison or on probation. Critics point to the murders of convicted sex offenders Joseph Gray (2006), William Elliott (2006), Michael Dodele (2007), Ray Pike (2008), and Walter Patey (2009) as proof that public lists of felons put a target on their backs.[13]

PAROLE

Most American convicts do not serve their full prison time. *Parole* ("spoken word," in French) allows early release of many inmates, in return for their agreement to abide by certain rules resembling those imposed by probation. Parole as it is practiced today began in 1840, with inmates of British penal colonies in Australia, and premiered in the United States at New York's Elmira Reformatory, under Warden Zebulon Brockway (1827–1920).

In modern America, state and federal laws determine the amount of time a convicted defendant must spend in custody before he or she is eligible for parole. Prison terms are either determinate (stating a specific period of time) or indeterminate (as in a sentence of "10 years to life"). Some sentences specify confinement without parole, but in all other cases, inmates may be considered for early release when a predetermined length of time has expired. Most states require that inmates serve roughly one-third of the term they receive from a judge, but standards vary between jurisdictions.

In order to receive parole, inmates must normally apply for release to a state parole board or commission. A hearing on the application will be scheduled and announced in advance. Many jurisdictions permit law enforcement officers, prosecutors, and an inmate's victims or their survivors to attend parole hearings and argue against release, while supporters may cite evidence of an inmate's reform and repentance. Eligibility for parole does not ensure that an inmate will be released.

Most states allow reduction of a convict's sentence for "good time," denoting periods of good behavior in custody. The rules of each state differ. Indiana, for example, deducts one day of "good time" for each day served in prison by a "Class I" inmate, one day for every two days served in "Class II," and no deduction for troublesome "Class III" inmates. Thus, a nonviolent felon sentenced to 10 years in prison may serve only five, if he or she obeys all disciplinary rules in the lockup.

LOVELLE MIXON

California felon Lovelle Mixon served five years in prison for assault with a deadly weapon, then spent another nine months inside for violating terms of his original parole. His second bid for freedom, beginning in November 2008, fared no better than the first. Mixon quarreled with his parole officer and missed several interviews. He skipped a final visit on March 22, 2009, embarking on a rampage that left four Oakland police officers dead.

The mayhem began at 1:15 P.M., when Sergeant Mark Dunakin and Officer John Hege stopped Mixon for a routine traffic violation. He shot both officers, leaving them dead in the street, and then fled to his sister's apartment on 74th Avenue. SWAT team officers found him there at 3:30 P.M. and laid siege to the apartment, removing Mixon's 16-year-old sister before another gun battle erupted. Mixon died in that exchange of fire, but not before he killed two more policemen: Sergeant Ervin Romans and Officer Daniel Sakai.

After the final shootout, Mixon's relatives blamed his parole officer for missing various scheduled meetings, a claim supervisors deemed "highly unlikely." Publication of Mixon's record disclosed that he was first paroled in October 2007, then placed "on hold" as a murder suspect in February 2008, and finally returned to prison for nine months after multiple parole violations. Released a second time on November 1, 2008, he was missing when his parole officer made home visits on February 18, 24, and 26.[14] Cases like Mixon's are the main reason why so many Americans today oppose parole for any inmate convicted of violent crimes.

"Good time" may be lost for disciplinary infractions, and inmate class-status is subject to periodic reviews.[15]

In December 2007 a total of 824,365 adult Americans were on parole nationwide. Nearly all (96 percent) had drawn sentences of one year or more, and 37 percent had served time for drug-related offenses. Eighty-eight percent of all parolees were men; 42 percent were white, 37 percent were African American, and 19 percent were Hispanic. At various times during 2007, a total of 1,180,469 parolees faced the risk of returning to prison for violating terms of their release, but only 16 percent of that group were actually incarcerated.[16]

Nationwide, five state agencies accounted for roughly half of all paroled inmates in 2006 (the last year with statistics available). California led the field with 125,067, Texas supervised 101,175 parolees, New York had 53,215 inmates at large, Illinois counted 33,354, and Pennsylvania claimed 24,956 parolees.[17]

Many prosecutors, law enforcement officers, and average U.S. citizens oppose parole today because of inmate recidivism—new offenses committed by inmates after their parole. A survey conducted by the Bureau of Justice Statistics, spanning the years 1986–1997, found that 11.4 percent of all federal prison inmates paroled during 1986, and 18.6 percent of those paroled in 1994, returned to prison within three years of their release. Sixty percent of those were locked up for technical violation of their parole terms, while 30 percent committed new crimes, and 10 percent returned to prison for unspecified "other violations." Thirty-two percent of violent felons returned to prison within three years, compared to 17 percent of those who committed property crimes, 15 percent of those held for public-order offenses, and 13 percent of drug-related offenders.[18]

Prison Rights
and Wrongs

Crescent City, California

Pelican Bay State Prison opened in 1989 as California's supermax facility for high-risk inmates. Located 370 miles north of San Francisco, near the Oregon border, it was designed to hold 2,550 prisoners but currently houses more than 3,300—nearly all of them classified as "Level IV" problem inmates.[1] Unfortunately, Pelican Bay has also had problems with some of its guards.

In September 1993 federal judge Thelton Henderson visited Pelican Bay to investigate claims of abuse filed by inmates. A disturbance broke out, with shots fired by guards who later displayed 26 homemade knives seized from inmates allegedly plotting to murder the judge. Further investigation proved that two guards—Jose Garcia and Edward Powers—staged the event to show Judge Henderson that Pelican Bay was a dangerous place, where force was required to control the inmates.[2]

FBI agents later charged Garcia and Powers with conspiracy to violate the civil rights of various inmates at Pelican Bay, charging that the two guards assaulted prisoners, encouraged other inmates to attack convicts Garcia and Powers disliked, and asked another guard to "look away" while an inmate was stabbed on their orders. At trial, in May 2002, jurors convicted both guards of conspiring to violate the Eighth Amendment's ban on cruel and unusual punishment. Garcia was acquitted on one count of arranging an inmate's beating by other convicts, and using the attack as an excuse to shoot the victim with a

37mm tear-gas gun. Garcia was sentenced to six years and four months in federal prison, while Powers received a seven-year sentence.[3]

When their trial judge refused to grant bail pending legal appeals, Garcia and Powers took their case to the Ninth Circuit U.S. Court of Appeals, which reversed that judgment in August 2003. Both defendants lost their subsequent appeals and were ordered to prison on October 2004. Jose Garcia died from cancer in March 2009, at a U.S. prison hospital in Butner, North Carolina. Powers remained in custody at the time of this writing, scheduled for release from his Florida prison in November 2012.

DEFINING RIGHTS

The Declaration of Independence states that all Americans have the right to "life, liberty, and pursuit of happiness," but convicted felons often lose their liberty—and some lose their lives—as a result of crimes they have committed. Once in prison, inmates also lose their right to privacy, except during communication with their lawyers. They are subject to round-the-clock observation by guards, and their mail is routinely opened for security reasons.

What rights, then, remain for criminal suspects and prison inmates?

The U.S. Constitution's Fourth Amendment protects all citizens against "unreasonable searches and seizures," requiring legal warrants issued by a court "upon probable cause, supported by Oath or affirmation, and particularly describing the place to be searched, and the persons or things to be seized."[4] Even so, suspects may be arrested without warrants in many situations—as when officers observe a crime in progress—and warrantless searches may be permitted under various circumstances defined by law and court rulings.

The Fifth Amendment roughly outlines procedures for a criminal *indictment* (formal charges), while stating that no person may be forced to confess any crime. It also bans *double jeopardy* (multiple trials for one offense) and states that no person may be "deprived of life, liberty, or property, without due process of law." The Sixth Amendment guarantees a "speedy" public trial by jury (though defendants may waive jury trials in most cases), and assures defendants of legal counsel.

The Eighth Amendment bans "excessive" bail or fines, along with "cruel and unusual punishment."[5]

Those broad rules allow for much leeway in legal proceedings. Trials may be delayed for months or years at the request of either side, and defendants who cannot afford bail may spend that time in jail. If convicted, they may (or may not) be given credit for time served prior to trial—but if acquitted, they receive no compensation for lost time. Further years of appeals may be required to determine if fines are "excessive," or whether specific punishments—including death—are "cruel and unusual." Even double jeopardy is flexible. Defendants acquitted of murder in state court, for instance, may later be convicted by a federal court on separate charges of violating their victim's civil right to life.

American courts have ruled that pretrial defendants who cannot afford bail must be housed in "humane" facilities, and that they may not be "punished" or treated as guilty before they are convicted. Even then, all prison inmates still enjoy protection from "cruel and unusual punishment" under the Eighth Amendment. In the 1878 case of *Wilkerson v. Utah,* the U.S. Supreme Court banned punishments such as "drawing and quartering, disemboweling alive, beheading, public dissecting, and burning alive."[6] Later rulings forbid the government from canceling a native-born American's citizenship (*Trop v. Dulles,* 1958), jailing drug users for their addiction (*Robinson v. California,* 1962), imposing jail terms "disproportionate" to an offense (*Solem v. Helms,* 1983), and executing the mentally handicapped (*Atkins v. Virginia,* 2002) or minors (*Roper v. Simmons,* 2005).

Other inmate rights, established through lawsuits filed by prisoners during the 20th century, include the following:

- protection from sexual assault or harassment
- adequate health care for both short-term and long-term illness
- equal access to facilities and programs for physically disabled inmates
- legal hearings prior to transfer of inmates from prison to a mental hospital
- freedom from racial segregation, except where required to stop violence

- freedom to complain about prison conditions and file lawsuits to correct them[7]

While those rights remain in effect, they are restricted by legal procedures. Convicts must exhaust internal prison grievance procedures before they file a lawsuit in federal court, and must then pay their own court filing fees. If the court dismisses an inmate's lawsuit as *malicious* (spiteful) or *frivolous* (unworthy of serious consideration), a "strike" may be logged against the inmate. Collection of three strikes may bar an inmate from filing further lawsuits, unless it is shown that he faces a real threat of death or serious injury. An inmate may lose "good time" accumulated toward parole if a judge determines that he or she filed a

HENRI THEODORE YOUNG (1918–?)

In 1995 critics praised a film titled *Murder in the First,* the "true story" of Alcatraz inmate Henri Young. According to the movie, Young stole $5 from a U.S. post office at age 17, to feed his starving sister, and was sent to Leavenworth Penitentiary, then transferred to Alcatraz. There, he tries to escape with inmate Rufus McCain, but is caught and placed in solitary confinement for three years, tortured by The Rock's sadistic warden (Gary Oldman). The torture drives Young insane, and he stabs McCain with a spoon, facing trial for first-degree murder. A young lawyer (Christian Slater) "saves" Young by getting the charge reduced to involuntary manslaughter, but Young returns to Alcatraz and its dungeon, where he dies in 1942 after scrawling "Victory" on the wall of his cell. The warden is later fired for brutality.

Actor Kevin Bacon won a Critics Choice Award for his portrayal of Young, while *Murder in the First* won a Human Rights Award from the Political Film Society—but was the story true?

In fact, while Henri Young *was* an orphan with a younger sister, he became a teenage bank robber and killed his first victim at age 15. He was never at Leavenworth, but served time in Montana and Washington state prisons before lawsuit to harass officials, that the inmate lied under oath, or that he or she presented false information. Finally, inmates may not sue for mental or emotional distress without proof of a corresponding physical injury.[8]

DISFRANCHISEMENT

In most states, convicted felons are disfranchised—stripped of their right to vote—but regulations differ for each jurisdiction nationwide. Only two states, Maine and Vermont, allow convicts to vote from prison.[9]

The District of Columbia and 13 states allow convicts to vote as soon as they are released from jail or prison, whether or not they are

entering the federal system at McNeil Island, Washington, in 1935. Transferred to Alcatraz a year later, he tried to escape with Rufus McCain and notorious bandit Arthur "Dock" Barker in January 1939. Guards killed Barker and captured Young and McCain. Both served a few months in solitary—not dungeon torture chambers—and then were returned to the general prison population. In 1940 Young stabbed McCain with two knives he made in the prison workshop, receiving additional time for manslaughter.

Young remained at Alcatraz until 1948, when he was transferred to the Medical Center for Federal Prisoners at Springfield, Missouri. His federal sentence expired in 1954, and he was returned to Washington's state prison for a life term arising from his 1930s murder conviction. Released on parole in 1972, he vanished without a trace and was never apprehended. In theory, he might still be alive.

The movie's warden, "Milton Glenn," is a fictional character created by screenwriter Dan Gordon, whose other films include *Wyatt Earp* (1994) and *The Celestine Prophecy* (2006). No Alcatraz warden was ever convicted of abusing prisoners, and Young's 1941 murder trial did not close Alcatraz, as *Murder in the First* suggests. The Rock remained open for "business" until March 1963.

ATTICA PRISON RIOT

The news of George Jackson's death at San Quentin in 1971 sparked anger among African-American prison inmates nationwide in summer 1971. Convicts at New York's Attica Correctional Facility were already disgruntled by rules that limited each convict to one shower per week and one roll of toilet paper per month. On September 9 a riot erupted at Attica. More than 1,000 of the prison's 2,225 inmates ran wild, seizing 33 guards as hostages and issuing a list of demands for reform.[10]

Over the next four days, state officials agreed to 28 of the inmates' demands, but they refused amnesty (freedom from punishment) to the rioters. On September 13 Governor Nelson Rockefeller ordered state police to intervene and crush the riot. Officers lobbed tear gas into the prison courtyard at 9:46 A.M., and then opened fire on the crowded grounds with shotguns and high-powered rifles. When the shooting stopped two minutes later, 29 inmates and nine hostages lay dead, with 89 persons wounded. Nor did the violence stop there, as state police and prison guards swarmed through the yard, beating many inmates—including some of the wounded—in retaliation for the riot.[11]

Initial reports claimed that inmates had murdered the nine prison guards by slashing their throats, but autopsies proved that all had been shot by police. (Inmates *did* kill a 10th guard and four unpopular prisoners, early in the riot, for a total of 43 dead.) A special commission, created to investigate the Attica

still on parole. Those relatively lenient states include Hawaii, Illinois, Indiana, Massachusetts, Michigan, Montana, New Hampshire, North Dakota, Ohio, Oregon, Pennsylvania, Rhode Island, and Utah.[12]

Stricter rules apply in five other states, which require inmates to complete their parole before casting a ballot. Those states include California, Colorado, Connecticut, New York, and South Dakota.[13]

Eighteen states ban voting by defendants in custody, on parole, or on probation. They include Alaska, Arkansas, Georgia, Idaho, Iowa, rebellion, called the retaliation by guards and police "inexcusable," adding that "[w]ith the exception of Indian massacres in the late 19th century, the State Police assault which ended the four-day prison uprising was the bloodiest one-day encounter between Americans since the Civil War."[14]

After the riot, 62 inmates were charged with a total of 1,289 crimes, while one state trooper faced charges of reckless endangerment. Lawsuits filed by inmates who had suffered gunshot wounds and beatings dragged on through the courts until 2000, when state authorities settled those claims for $12 million. Another $12 million was paid in 2004 to survivors of the nine guards killed by state police gunfire.[15]

The yard of the Attica Correctional Facility is left in ruins in the aftermath of the September 1971 riot. *AP Photo*

Kansas, Louisiana, Maryland, Minnesota, Missouri, New Jersey, New Mexico, North Carolina, Oklahoma, South Carolina, Texas, West Virginia, and Wisconsin. Iowa inmates released since July 2005 must await restoration of their franchise by the governor "without undue delay," while Maryland requires full payment of any outstanding fines before an ex-convict can vote.[16]

The last 12 states maintain the strictest rules. Convicted felons must appeal to state or county authorities for restoration of their voting rights in Arizona, Florida, Kentucky, Mississippi, Nevada, Tennessee, Virginia, Washington, and Wyoming, and approval may be denied. Alabama permanently disfranchises persons convicted of murder, rape, incest, child-molestation, or treason. Nebraska, likewise, bans convicted traitors from voting for the remainder of their lives. Delaware felons must wait five years to vote after completion of their sentences, and violent criminals require a pardon from the governor. Second-time felons face the same restrictions in Wyoming, and five-year delays also apply to Virginia residents convicted of violent crimes, drug sales, or electoral offenses. Tennessee requires specific applications from persons convicted of murder, rape, treason, or voter fraud.[17]

While no ongoing census of disfranchised felons is maintained in America, a survey conducted in December 2004 found 5,259,530 persons—2.42 percent of the total U.S. electorate—banned from voting based on criminal convictions. That total included 1,315,387 confined to state and federal prisons, 62,878 lodged in local jails, 477,704 on parole, 1,344,883 on probation, and 2,058,678 ex-felons who had failed to meet various state requirements for voting. Florida led the nation with 1,179,687 felons disfranchised, while Texas came second with 522,887.[18]

DEFENDING INMATE RIGHTS

Countless lawsuits protest conditions inside America's jails and prison each year. The American Civil Liberties Union (ACLU) has filed many such cases, exposing conditions where inmates' rights were violated. Some of those cases include:

- *Maricopa County, Arizona*: In October 2008 a federal court found that the Maricopa County Jail, run by Sheriff Joe Arpaio, threatened inmate health and safety with rundown facilities, moldy food, and substandard medical care. Following that victory, ACLU spokesperson Margaret Winter told reporters, "Sheriff Arpaio's horrendous treatment of detainees, especially those with severe medical and mental health problems, has caused terrible suffering for years."[19]
- *Washington, D.C.*: In December 2008, ACLU attorneys won a large financial settlement for relatives of Jonathan Magbie, a

Inmates sit next to their bunks in the courtyard of Maricopa
County Sheriff Joe Arpaio's jail in Phoenix, Arizona. The prison
was long believed to be unsafe for prisoners, and in October 2008
a federal court ruled that the facility, its food, and its medical care
were substandard and detrimental to inmate health. *AP Photo/*
Charlie Riedel

quadriplegic inmate who died from pneumonia while serving a
10-day sentence at the Greater Southeast Community Hospital
for possession of a marijuana cigarette. The court found that
hospital attendants ignored Magbie's special needs, including a
tracheotomy tube and other breathing equipment required to
keep him alive.[20]

- *Washington, D.C.:* The ACLU opposed a new ban on "vital religious works," imposed by the Federal Bureau of Prisons in March
2009. The ban included confiscation of religious literature which,
in the opinion of prison officials, "could suggest" acts of violence
or other criminal behavior.[21]

- *Los Angeles*: Following the apparent suicide of a county jail inmate, the ACLU published a report in April 2009, documenting "how brutally overcrowded conditions cause or contribute to violence and serious mental illness in Los Angeles County's Aging Men's Central Jail." According to that report, the jail "is so grossly overcrowded, dangerous and dungeon-like that it puts intolerable stress on the jailed as well as the jailers."[22] Jailers disagreed.
- *Milwaukee, Wisconsin*: In April 2009, after three years of litigation, the ACLU obtained a court order requiring proper administration of medicine at the state's largest women's prison, Taycheedah Correctional Institution. Prior to that order, prescription drugs were dispensed by guards with no medical training, often on haphazard schedules.[23]

Many Americans believe that the ACLU and some courts are "too liberal" in defense of inmates' rights. They say that prisoners deserve no more than decent food and medical care—the bare necessities of life. They condemn luxuries such as cable TV in prisons—which cost the state of Oklahoma $280,000 in 2008—and athletic equipment that produces bigger, stronger felons.[24] The debate will certainly continue.

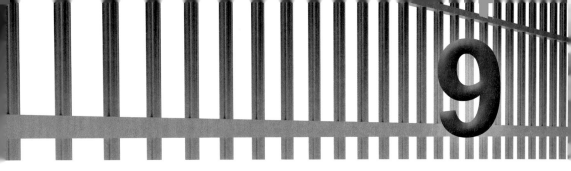

New World
Disorder

Milan, Italy

On February 17, 2003, Muslim clergyman Hassan Nasr was seized by agents of the U.S. Central Intelligence Agency (CIA) and driven to Milan's Malpensa Airport. A U.S. Army Special Air Resources jet flew Nasr to Ramstein, Germany, where another plane carried him onward to Cairo, Egypt. There, Nasr claims, he was held in jail and tortured in an effort to make him confess acts of terrorism. Italian police noted his disappearance and began an investigation.[1]

Nasr remained in Egypt until February 2007, when a court ruled the terror charges "unfounded." Meanwhile, Italian authorities issued arrest warrants for 13 alleged CIA agents in June 2005, expanded in December to include 22 suspects, with four more added in 2006.[2]

As the case dragged on, stalled by CIA denials, Italian police arrested two of their country's own intelligence officers in July 2006 for participation in Nasr's kidnapping. Secret memos surfaced, proving that Italy's Military Intelligence and Security Service had cooperated with the CIA. Twenty-six Americans and nine Italians finally faced trial in June 2007, but it was soon adjourned while Italy's Supreme Court reviewed the law concerning release of secret documents.[3]

The court eventually barred most government files related to Nasr's case from use as evidence in court. Prosecutors moved ahead with their case in May 2008, although convictions seemed unlikely. The sluggish case was still in progress a year later, when an attorney for one defendant told reporters, "We're continuing, but it is more of a formality."[4]

9/11

Life changed for most Americans on September 11, 2001. That morning 19 members of the terrorist group Al-Qaeda ("the base," in Arabic) hijacked four commercial airliners departing from Boston; Newark, New Jersey; and Washington, D.C., bound for Los Angeles and San Francisco. Aside from the hijackers, those planes carried 247 passengers and crew members.[5]

Between 8:46 and 9:03 A.M., two of the hijacked planes crashed into New York City's World Trade Center, destroying both high-rise towers. American Airlines Flight 77 struck the Pentagon, in Virginia, at 9:37 A.M. The fourth plane—United Airlines Flight 93, earmarked for the White House—crashed near Shanksville, Pennsylvania, at 10:03 A.M., while passengers fought with the hijackers. The final death toll stands at 2,973 American victims, plus all 19 terrorists.[6]

Sweeping changes followed the 9/11 attacks. Aside from heightened airport security, President George W. Bush reorganized America's federal law enforcement structure, creating a new Department of Homeland Security (DHS) to defend the nation against future attacks. Agencies formerly scattered in several cabinet departments—Treasury's Secret Service, the State Department's Immigration and Naturalization Service, the Department of Labor's Border Patrol, and the independent Customs Service—were lumped together within DHS, sometimes renamed and assigned to new missions. The CIA and FBI remained independent, while shifting priorities to emphasize counterterrorist activities above all others.

Congress responded to 9/11 by passing the USA PATRIOT Act (Uniting and Strengthening America by Providing Appropriate Tools Required to Intercept and Obstruct Terrorism) in October 2001. The new law eased or abolished many restrictions on spying by U.S. intelligence agencies, both at home and abroad, while granting federal agents broad authority to detain and deport immigrants suspected of terrorist activity.

And the Bush administration went further, still. In 2006 the Washington Post revealed that President Bush had authorized an illegal operation by the National Security Agency "to eavesdrop on telephone and e-mail communications between the United States and people overseas without a warrant."[7]

In the aftermath of 9/11 at least 1,200 Muslim aliens—some reports say 4,500—were detained nationwide as "suspected terrorists." None were charged with any crime, although some remained in custody for over a year. No statistics are available on the number finally deported, since the detentions and subsequent proceedings were carried out in secret, without legal counsel for the accused.[8]

Pursuit of terrorists, even when none are found, is time-consuming business. Soon after 9/11, FBI Director Robert Mueller III announced that his agency would focus most of its attention on counterterrorism, while cutting back investigations of other federal offenses, including narcotics trafficking, racketeering and white-collar crime. A survey conducted by Syracuse University in December 2001 found that FBI referrals of "ordinary" criminals for federal prosecution had dropped 76 percent from the totals seen in 2000. Critics of the change complain that single-minded pursuit of invisible terrorists permits other dangerous felons to operate freely.[9]

"GITMO"

The U.S. Navy built a base at Cuba's Guantanamo Bay—nicknamed "Gitmo"—in 1898, and secured a 99-year lease on the property in 1903. That lease expired in 2002, and while Cuba's present government considers America's presence illegal, Cuba's army lacks the strength to expel U.S. forces.

During 2002 America established a detention facility for suspected foreign terrorists at Guantanamo Bay. The lockup consisted of three camps—called "Delta," "Iguana," and "X-Ray"—housing prisoners captured after the American invasions of Afghanistan and Iraq. An executive order signed by President Bush in 2001 allowed the military to hold foreign prisoners of war indefinitely without filing criminal charges. The Department of Justice also declared that since Gitmo lies outside the United States, inmates are not entitled to legal counsel or other constitutional rights. President Bush also denied the inmates protection under the Geneva Conventions—treaties guaranteeing that

A soldier opens a gate on the grounds of the maximum security prison at Camp Delta 2 and 3 at the Guantanamo Bay U.S. Naval Base in April 2006. *AP Photo/Brennan Linsley*

prisoners of war "shall in all circumstances be treated humanely," banning "outrages upon personal dignity, in particular humiliating and degrading treatment."[10]

Those moves prompted criticism in America and around the world. On June 29, 2006, in the case of *Hamdan v. Rumsfeld,* the U.S. Supreme Court ruled that Gitmo detainees *are* entitled to basic rights under the Geneva Conventions. Available statistics indicate that Gitmo held 775 prisoners at peak capacity; 420 of those were later freed with no charges filed, while 245 remained in January 2009. The discrepancy of 110 remains unexplained, but an uncertain number of prisoners died in confinement, including several reported suicides.[11]

EXTRAORDINARY RENDITION

Most international terrorists operate outside of American territory, frustrating efforts to arrest them when they hide in neutral countries or nations hostile to America. To overcome that obstacle, beginning in the 1980s the U.S. government adopted the practice of kidnapping suspects from foreign soil and transporting them to America or other friendly nations for trial. In federal jargon, such kidnappings are called "extraordinary rendition."

The first known case occurred in October 1985, when terrorists hijacked the Italian cruise ship *Achille Lauro* and killed an American tourist. The killers negotiated safe passage to Tunis, aboard an Egyptian aircraft, but President Ronald Reagan sent air force jets to divert the plane and force a landing in Sicily. Four of the gunmen were tried, convicted, and sentenced to prison for murder.

Two years later, in September 1987, the FBI and CIA ran "Operation Goldenrod," to capture Lebanese terrorist Fawaz Yunis. Agents lured him from hiding with offers of a drug deal, seized him on a yacht in the Mediterranean, and returned him to America for trial, where he received a 30-year sentence.

President Bill Clinton continued the rendition policy. Counterterrorism advisor Richard Clarke proposed an abduction in 1993, prompting Vice President Al Gore to say, "Of course it's a violation of international law, that's why it's a covert action. The guy is a terrorist. Go grab [him]."[12] Two years later, in June 1995, Clinton issued a presidential directive authorizing CIA abduction of fugitive terrorists.[13]

Extraordinary rendition accelerated after 9/11, with a significant change. Instead of bringing terrorists back to the United States for trial, agents placed them aboard secret "ghost flights" and flew them to countries where torture is commonly used to obtain information from criminal suspects. By June 2006 the Council of Europe estimated that 100 persons had been snatched from European soil.[14] Eight months later, the European Parliament reported that 1,245 CIA flights had passed through Europe, carrying prisoners to nations where torture is practiced.[15]

ENHANCED INTERROGATION

Use of torture since 9/11 has not been restricted to America's foreign allies. Government memos and other evidence collected since 2001 prove that President Bush approved CIA use of "enhanced interrogation," also dubbed "rough," "harsh," and "alternative" interrogation. In a speech delivered in September 2006, President Bush described the interrogation of terrorist suspect Abu Zubaydah as follows:

ABU GHRAIB

Iraq's Central Prison is located 20 miles west of Baghdad, in the town of Abu Ghraib ("place of ravens"). Dictator Saddam Hussein (1937–2006) filled it with his political opponents and members of Iraq's Kurdish minority until 2003, when the U.S. Army's 320th Military Police Battalion seized the facility, replacing its former inmates with alleged terrorists or "insurgents." By 2004 rumors of prisoner abuse including torture, sexual assault, and murder began emerging from Abu Ghraib, prompting investigation by CBS News and journalist Seymour Hersh.[16]

Those investigations—and subsequent military inquiries—revealed a pattern of abuse at Abu Ghraib, including beatings, maulings by attack dogs, and sexual humiliation of inmates, all documented by photographs and videotapes. While some 90 percent of Abu Ghraib's inmates were found innocent of any crime, 17 American officers and soldiers were removed from duty at the prison, with 13 facing criminal charges. Between May 2004 and September 2005, 12 defendants received varying degrees of punishment.[17] They included:

- Colonel Thomas Pappas, fined $8,000 on two counts of dereliction of duty, plus a General Officer Memorandum of Reprimand that effectively ended his career
- Lieutenant Colonel Steven Jordan, acquitted of criminal charges but reprimanded for disobeying orders to keep silent about the investigation
- Specialist Charles Graner, sentenced to 10 years for conspiracy to maltreat detainees, failure to protect detainees from abuse, cruelty, maltreatment, assault, indecency, adultery, and obstruction of justice

As his questioning proceeded, it became clear that he had received training on how to resist interrogation. And so the CIA used an alternative set of procedures. These procedures were designed to

- Private Lynndie England, eight years on four counts of mal-treating prisoners, two counts of conspiracy, and one count of dereliction of duty, paroled after serving 571 days
- Staff Sergeant Ivan Frederick, eight years, plus demotion to private, and a dishonorable discharge for conspiracy, der-eliction, maltreatment of detainees, assault, and committing an indecent act
- Sergeant Javal Davis, six months, plus demotion to private, and a bad-conduct discharge for dereliction, making false official statements, and battery
- Specialist Armin Cruz, eight months, plus demotion to pri-vate, and a bad-conduct discharge in exchange for testi-mony as a prosecution witness
- Specialist Sabrina Harman, six months and a bad-conduct discharge on six felony counts
- Specialist Megan Ambuhl, demoted to private and docked two weeks' pay for dereliction of duty
- Sergeant Santos Cardona, 90 days for dereliction of duty and aggravated assault. Cardona retained his rank and was later sent to Kuwait, where he trains Iraqi police
- Specialist Roman Krol, 10 months, demotion to private, and a bad-conduct discharge for conspiracy and maltreatment of detainees
- Sergeant Michael Smith, 179 days, a $2,250 fine, demotion to private, and a bad-conduct discharge for two counts of prisoner maltreatment, one count of simple assault, one count of conspiracy to maltreat, one count of dereliction of duty, and a final charge of an indecent act

While charged with no crimes, Abu Ghraib's commander, Brigadier General Janis Karpinsky, was removed from her post in April 2008 and demoted to colonel in May. Her demo-tion was not officially related to the prison scandal. Karpinsky describes it as political persecution.[18]

GHOST FLIGHTS

Despite secret approval from Washington, extraordinary rendition is still a crime in countries where criminal suspects are kidnapped by U.S. agents. Therefore, prisoners cannot be transported between nations on official aircraft or aboard civilian commercial flights. To carry out abductions secretly, the CIA conducted "ghost flights"—using aircraft with false registrations and flight plans—to shuttle prisoners around the world while preserving government "deniability."

The first public notice of ghost flights occurred in Spain, whose government launched an investigation in November 2005. Jose Antonio Alonso, Spain's Minister of the Interior, told British journalists that Spanish police had traced at least 10 secret CIA flights in and out of Son Sant Joan airport between January 22, 2004, and January 17, 2005, with destinations including Algeria, Djibouti, Ireland, Libya, Macedonia, Morocco, Romania, Sweden, and Washington, D.C.[19]

Two weeks later, the *Toronto Star* revealed that CIA aircraft were also shuttling in and out of Canada on "ghost" missions, using planes registered to fictitious "shell companies" with false addresses and telephone numbers. Canadian authorities reacted angrily to the news, remembering the case of

be safe, to comply with our laws, our Constitution, and our treaty obligations. The Department of Justice reviewed the authorized methods extensively and determined them to be lawful. I cannot describe the specific methods used . . . But I can say the procedures were tough, and they were safe, and lawful, and necessary.[20]

Today, we know that those techniques included "waterboarding"—simulated drowning—and suspicion persists that even more extreme techniques were used.[21] Unverified rumors of fatal interrogations persist from Guantanamo Bay, and one subject—Iraqi Major General Abed Mowhoush—died in November 2003 from repeated beatings inflicted by U.S. Army interrogators.[22]

Ottawa resident Maher Arar, who was kidnapped from New York's John F. Kennedy Airport in September 2002, flown to Syria, and tortured as a "terrorist suspect" for 374 days before his release. That incident inspired the 2007 film *Rendition,* starring Reese Witherspoon, Jake Gyllenhall, and Meryl Streep.[24]

Amnesty International, a group that protests mistreatment of political prisoners worldwide, issued a report on the CIA's ghost flights and torture in February 2006. It revealed that prisoners kidnapped abroad were flown to CIA "black sites"—secret prisons—under a directive signed by President Bush in September 2001. Black sites operated in nations where torture is routine, including Egypt, Jordan, Morocco, Pakistan, Qatar, Saudi Arabia, and Syria. Hundreds of flights had transported an uncertain number of victims from airports in Britain, Germany, Iceland, Spain, Sweden, and Switzerland. At least 50 "rendition" flights had landed at Ireland's Shannon Airport alone, although U.S. Secretary of State Condoleezza Rice assured Irish officials that Shannon had not been used for any "untoward" (unfavorable) activities. Martin Scheinin, spokesman for the United Nations Commission on Human Rights, noted, "It isn't unusual that governments deny involvement and try to keep it secret as long as possible."[25]

Such methods are banned by the Geneva Conventions, the 1948 United Nations Universal Declaration of Human Rights, and the 1987 United Nations Convention Against Torture and Other Cruel, Inhuman or Degrading Treatment or Punishment. However, Attorney General Alberto Gonzales dismissed the Geneva Conventions as "quaint" (amusingly old-fashioned) in 2003, while President Bush demanded exemption for U.S. soldiers from trial as war criminals—a move abandoned due to international protests in June 2004.[23]

Widespread denunciation of "enhanced interrogation" prompted the White House to defend its stance, while arguing over the definition of "torture." In January 2009 government spokesperson Susan Crawford said that techniques used at Guantanamo Bay "were all authorized, but the manner in which they applied them was overly aggressive and too persistent."[26]

Four months later, ex-Vice President Dick Cheney said that he had "no regrets" over use of rough interrogation methods, adding, "I think it was absolutely the right thing to do. I'm convinced, absolutely convinced, that we saved thousands, perhaps hundreds of thousands of lives." Pressed to describe a case where torture prevented terrorist attacks, Cheney refused "because it's still classified."[27]

President Barack Obama signed an executive order banning torture on January 22, 2009. The same order suspended military trials at Guantanamo Bay for six months, and declared that the detention camp would close before year's end. At the time of this writing the camp remained open and the future status of its detainees unclear.

Chronology

1608	First colonial execution carried out in Virginia, for espionage
1611	The Virginia Company in London drafts the first colonial criminal laws
1647	First execution for witchcraft, in Connecticut
1691–1796	New York courts impose a total of 19 prison sentences
1733	Early Georgia colonists include many inmates from British debtors' prisons
1768	First U.S. debtors' prison opens in Tappahannock, Virginia
1773	Connecticut establishes Newgate Prison at Simsbury
1776	Quakers organize the Philadelphia Society for Alleviating Distressed Prisoners
1790	Connecticut's Newgate Prison becomes the first American state prison; Walnut Street Jail opens in Philadelphia, Pennsylvania
1791	The Bill of Rights establishes broad guidelines for criminal trials and punishment
1797	New York opens Newgate Prison in Greenwich Village, New York City
1817	Auburn State Penitentiary opens in Auburn, New York
1819	Whipping up to 39 lashes authorized at Auburn State Penitentiary
1821	Solitary confinement begins as discipline at Auburn State Penitentiary
1824	New York opens a House of Refuge for juvenile offenders deemed reformable

1825   Sing Sing Prison opens at Ossining, New York

1829   Eastern State Penitentiary opens in Philadelphia

1833   Federal imprisonment for debt is restricted; most states follow suit

1839   Mount Pleasant Prison for women opens at Ossining, New York

1841   Judge John Augustus pioneers probation in Boston, Massachusetts

1851   California's first state prison opens on the *Waban*, anchored in San Francisco Bay

1852   San Quentin State Prison opens near San Rafael, California

1855   Michigan opens a House of Corrections for juvenile offenders

1858   Joliet Correctional Center opens at Joliet, Illinois

1859   New York State Asylum for Insane Convicts opens at Auburn, New York

1864   109 Union prisoners escape from Libby Prison in Richmond, Virginia

1865–1866   Southern states restore de facto slavery with "Black Codes"

1868   Georgia inaugurates the convict lease system

1870   National Congress on Penitentiary and Reform Discipline founded

1875   Military prison opens at Fort Leavenworth, Kansas; first federal prisoners received at McNeil Island, Washington

1876   Elmira Reformatory opens in Elmira, New York

1888   Illinois establishes America's first juvenile court

1890   First execution by electric chair, at Sing Sing Prison

1891   Congress passes the Three Prisons Act

1895   Fort Leavenworth begins conversion into first U.S. federal prison

1899   First female prisoner executed by electric chair, at Sing Sing Prison

1901 Reformatory for Women opens at Bedford Hills, New York

1902 U.S. Penitentiary opens in Atlanta, Georgia

1904 McNeil Island officially becomes a federal prison

1920 New York pioneers indefinite sentencing for "mentally defective" prisoners

1925 Stateville Correctional Center opens in Crest Hill, Illinois

1927 Alderson Federal Prison for women opens at Alderson, West Virginia

1928 Alabama is the last state to outlaw convict leasing

1929 Auburn, New York, prison riot

1930 Congress establishes the Federal Bureau of Prisons; 320 inmates die in fire at Ohio State Prison in Columbus

1931 Joliet, Illinois, prison riot

1932 California Institution for Women opens at Tehachapi

1934 U.S. Penitentiary opens on Alcatraz Island, in San Francisco Bay, California

1962 Three inmates apparently escape from Alcatraz

1963 U.S. Penitentiary opens at Marion, Illinois, replacing Alcatraz

1967 Fire at Florida's Jay Prison Camp claims 37 lives

1969 *Johnson v. Avery* permits inmates to act as jailhouse lawyers for other convicts

1971 Riot at New York's Attica Correctional Facility claims 39 lives; six die in rioting at California's San Quentin State Prison

1972 *Furman v. Georgia* holds existing U.S. capital punishment laws unconstitutional

1973 Oklahoma State Penitentiary riot

1976 *Gregg v. Georgia* permits executions to resume under new guidelines

1977 *Bounds v. Smith* requires prisons to maintain law libraries for inmates

1978 U.S. Penitentiary at Marion, Illinois, becomes the first American "supermax" prison

1979 *Bell v. Wolfish* permits invasive searches of inmates held pending trial

1980 New Mexico State Penitentiary riot claims 30 lives

1982 First U.S. execution by lethal injection, in Texas

1983 Georgia establishes the first "boot camp" for young offenders

1985 First publicized use of "extraordinary rendition" against foreign fugitives

1986 America's first privately owned prison opens in Kentucky

1987 *Turner v. Safley* affirms inmate freedom of religion

1992 *Hudson v. McMillan* bans excessive force to maintain prison discipline

1994 Congress establishes "truth-in-sentencing" for violent crimes

1995 Alabama, Arizona, and Florida reintroduce chain gangs

1997 New federal regulations permit violent juveniles to be housed in adult prisons

1997 First of many misconduct scandals involving private prisons in Texas

2002 Guantanamo Bay Detention Camp established in Cuba for suspected terrorists

2004 Abu Ghraib military prison scandal in Iraq

2006 President George W. Bush acknowledges CIA secret prisons abroad

2009 President Barack Obama closes foreign CIA "black sites"

Endnotes

Introduction

1. Federal Bureau of Investigation, "Uniform Crime Report," http://www.fbi.gov/ucr/ucr.htm (Accessed October 22, 2009).
2. *Ibid.*
3. Jack Shafer, "Crazy about guns," Slate, http://www.slate.com/id/2204592 (Accessed October 22, 2009).
4. "Honoring Officers Killed in the Year 2009," Officer Down Memorial Page, http://www.odmp.org/year.php (Accessed October 24, 2009).
5. Bureau of Justice Statistics, "Corrections Statistics," http://www.ojp.usdoj.gov/bjs/correct.htm (Accessed October 22, 2009).

Chapter 1

1. Corinne Reilly, "USP Atwater Correctional Officer's Death Shines Light on Faulty System," *Merced* (Calif.) *Sun-Star,* June 2, 2009.
2. *Ibid.*
3. *Ibid.*
4. "Prison Nation," *New York Times,* March 10, 2008.
5. Roy Walmsley, "World Prison Population List," 8th ed., International Centre for Prison Studies, http://www.kcl.ac.uk/depsta/law/research/icps/downloads/wppl-8th_41.pdf (Accessed October 24, 2009).

6. *Ibid.*
7. Bureau of Justice Statistics, "Correction Statistics," http://www.ojp.usdoj.gov/bjs/correct.htm (Accessed October 24, 2009).
8. "Prison Nation," *New York Times,* March 10, 2008.
9. Bureau of Justice Statistics, "Correction Statistics," http://www.ojp.usdoj.gov/bjs/correct.htm (Accessed October 24, 2009).
10. *Ibid.*
11. Death Penalty Information Center, "Facts About the Death Penalty," http://www.deathpenaltyinfo.org/documents/FactSheet.pdf (Accessed October 24, 2009).
12. "Insanity and the Law," Florida International University, http://www.fiu.edu/~cohne/Theory%20S09/Ch%206%20-%20Insanity%20and%20the%20Law.pdf (Accessed October 24, 2009).
13. *Ibid.*
14. Joan Biskupic, "Court: Insanity Defense Not a Right," *Washington Post,* March 29, 1994.
15. Bureau of Justice Statistics, "Correction Statistics," http://www.ojp.usdoj.gov/bjs/correct.htm (Accessed October 24, 2009).
16. Death Penalty Information Center, "Facts About the Death Penalty," http://www.deathpenaltyinfo.

org/documents/FactSheet.pdf (Accessed October 24, 2009).

17. U.S. Constitution, Amendment VIII.

18. "Lee Malvo's Rights," Constitution-and-rights.com, http://www.constitution-and-rights.com/rights-4.html (Accessed October 24, 2009).

19. "Prison Privatization and Use of Incarceration," The Sentencing Project, http://www.sentencingproject.org/Admin/Documents/publications/inc_prisonprivatization.pdf (Accessed October 24, 2009); Geoffrey Segal, "Increased Competition in Department of Corrections Will Lead to Additional Savings," *Virginia Viewpoint* (June 2003), http://www.virginiainstitute.org/viewpoint/2003_08.html (Accessed October 24, 2009).

Chapter 2

1. Charles Suters, "Ohio's Prison Horror," in *Disaster!*, Ben Kartman, ed. (New York: Pellegrini & Cudahy, 1948), 220.

2. *Ibid.*, 221–2.

3. *Ibid.*, 223–4.

4. "A List of Victims of the Ohio Penitentiary Fire," Ohio American Local History Network, http://www.genealogybug.net/ohio_alhn/crime/ohio_pen_fire.html (Accessed October 24, 2009).

5. "This Day in History," History.com, April 21, 1930, http://www.history.com/this-day-in-history.do?action=Article&id=410 (Accessed October 24, 2009).

6. "Prison History," Law Library, http://law.jrank.org/pages/1786/Prisons-History.html (Accessed October 24, 2009).

7. "Executions in the U.S. 1608-2002," Death Penalty Information Center, http://www.deathpenalty-info.org/ESPYyear.pdf (Accessed October 24, 2009).

8. "Prison History," Law Library, http://law.jrank.org/pages/1786/Prisons-History.html (Accessed October 24, 2009).

9. Declaration of Independence.

10. "Prison History," Law Library, http://law.jrank.org/pages/1786/Prisons-History.html (Accessed October 24, 2009).

11. *Ibid.*

12. *Ibid.*

13. *Exodus* 22:18 and *Leviticus* 20:27.

14. "Executions in the U.S. 1608–2002," Death Penalty Information Center, http://www.deathpenaltyinfo.org/ESPYyear.pdf (Accessed October 24, 2009); Historical Witches and Witchtrials in North America, http://www.personal.utulsa.edu/~Marc-Carlson/witchtrial/na.html (Accessed October 24, 2009).

15. "Executions in the U.S. 1608–2002," Death Penalty Information Center, http://www.deathpenalty-info.org/ESPYyear.pdf (Accessed October 24, 2009)

16. "Prison History," Law Library, http://law.jrank.org/pages/1786/Prisons-History.html (Accessed October 24, 2009).

17. "Andersonville Prison," Civil War Prisons, http://www.civilwarhome.com/andersonville.htm (Accessed October 24, 2009).

18. Historical Witches and Witchtrials in North America, http://www.personal.utulsa.edu/~Marc-Carlson/witchtrial/

na.html (Accessed October 24, 2009).

19. *Ibid.*

20. Randall Shelden, "Slavery in the Third Millennium," The Black Commentator, http://blackcom-mentator.com/142/142_slavery_2.html (Accessed October 24, 2009).

21. "Prison History," Law Library, http://law.jrank.org/pages/1786/Prisons-History.html (Accessed October 24, 2009).

22. "Elmira," New York Correction History Society, http://www.cor-rectionhistory.org/html/chronicl/docs2day/elmira.html (Accessed November 2, 2009).

23. "Excellence in Corrections," Cor-rections Corporation of America, http://www.correctionscorp.com (Accessed October 24, 2009).

24. "About Cornell Companies, Inc," Cornell Companies, http://www.cornellcompanies.com/pages/aboutcornell.html (Accessed October 24, 2009).

25. "Who We Are," The Geo Group, http://www.thegeogroupinc.com/about.asp (Accessed October 24, 2009).

26. "About CEC," Community Educa-tion Centers, http://www.cecintl.com/About/default.aspx (Accessed October 24, 2009).

27. Erin Rosa, "Crashing Economy Works Well for Private Prisons," War is Crime.com, http://www.wariscrime.com/2009/06/04/news/crashing-economy-works-well-for-private-prisons (Accessed October 24, 2009).

28. "Prison History," Law Library, http://law.jrank.org/pages/1786/Prisons-History.html (Accessed October 24, 2009).

29. "Past Scandals and Problems with Private Prisons," Texas Prison Bid'ness, http://www.texasprison-bidness.org/about-private-prisons/past-scandals-and-problems-private-prisons (Accessed October 24, 2009).

30. *Ibid.*

31. Public Services International Research Unit, "Prison Privatisa-tion Report International," http://www.psiru.org/justice/PPRI74W.htm#UnitedStates (Accessed Octo-ber 24, 2009).

32. Rosa, "Crashing Economy."

33. Prison Privatisation Report International.

34. *Ibid.*

35. George Monbiot, "This Revolting Trade in Human Lives Is an Incen-tive to Lock People Up," *The Guard-ian* (London), March 3, 2009.

36. "A Brief History of the Bureau of Prisons," Federal Bureau of Pris-ons, http://www.bop.gov/about/history.jsp (Accessed November 2, 2009).

37. Morgan O. Reynolds, "Factories Behind Bars," National Center for Policy Analysis, http://www.ncpa.org/pub/st206 (Accessed October 24, 2009).

38. "Prison History," Law Library, http://law.jrank.org/pages/1786/Prisons-History.html (Accessed October 24, 2009).

39. *Ibid.*; "Correctional Populations in the United States, 1994," Bureau of Justice Statistics, http://www.ojp.usdoj.gov/bjs/abstract/cpius94.htm (Accessed November 2, 2009).

Chapter 3

1. "Number of Cities in the U.S.," National League of Cities, http://

www.nlc.org/about_cities/
cities_101/138.aspx (Accessed
October 24, 2009); U.S. Census
Bureau, http://censtats.census.gov/
usa/usainfo.shtml (Accessed October 24, 2009).

2. "Jail statistics," Bureau of Justice
Statistics, http://www.ojp.usdoj.
gov/bjs/jails.htm (Accessed October 24, 2009).

3. *Ibid.*

4. *Ibid.*; "Fact Sheet," U.S. Census
Bureau, http://factfinder.census.
gov/servlet/ACSSAFFFacts?_
submenuId=factsheet_0&_sse=on
(Accessed October 24, 2009).

5. "Fact Sheet," U.S. Census
Bureau, http://factfinder.census.
gov/servlet/ACSSAFFFacts?_
submenuId=factsheet_0&_sse=on
(Accessed October 27, 2009); "Jail
Statistics," Bureau of Justice Statistics, http://www.ojp.usdoj.gov/bjs/
jails.htm (Accessed October 24,
2009).

6. "Jail statistics," Bureau of Justice
Statistics, http://www.ojp.usdoj.
gov/bjs/jails.htm (Accessed October 24, 2009).

7. "Department of Corrections,"
Cook County Sheriff, http://
www.cookcountysheriff.org/doc/
doc_main.html (Accessed October
24, 2009).

8. *Ibid.*

9. *Ibid.*

10. Monica Davey, "Federal Report
Finds Poor Conditions at Cook
County Jail," *New York Times,* July
18, 2008.

11. *Ibid.*

12. Manuel Roig-Franzia and Melanie
Lasoff Levs, "3 Slain in Atlanta
Courthouse Rampage," *Washing-
ton Post,* March 12, 2005.

13. *Ibid.*

14. "Jail statistics," Bureau of Justice
Statistics, http://www.ojp.usdoj.
gov/bjs/jails.htm (Accessed October 24, 2009).

15. *Ibid.*

16. *Ibid.*

17. *Ibid.*

18. *Ibid.*

19. Ben Winslow, "2 More Deputies
Resign in Jail Scandal," *Deseret
Morning News* (Salt Lake City),
April 5, 2006.

20. "Prison Scandal Timeline," *Pocono
Record,* June 11, 2009; David
Pierce, "Troubles Continue at
Monroe County jail," *Pocono
Record,* March 2, 2009; "Mon-
roe Corrections Officer Fired in
Wake of Inmate's Suicide," *Pocono
Record,* May 6, 2009.

21. "Jail Scandal," NBC News, February 27, 2009; Angela Brown, "Ex-
sheriff in Jail Sex Scandal Dies,"
Abilene (Texas) *Reporter News,*
May 2, 2009.

Chapter 4

1. "Correctional Facility Directory,"
Alabama Department of Corrections, http://www.doc.state.
al.us/docs/DOCAddressPhones.
pdf (Accessed October 24,
2009); "Division of Institutions,"
Alaska Department of Corrections, http://www.correct.state.
ak.us/corrections/institutions/
institutions.jsf (Accessed October
24, 2009); "CDCR Prisons and
Conservation Camps," California
Department of Corrections, http://
www.cdcr.ca.gov/Prisons/index.
html (Accessed October 24, 2009).

2. Hawaii Department of Public
Safety, http://hawaii.gov/psd/

corrections (Accessed October 24, 2009).

3. Bureau of Justice Statistics, "Prison Statistics," http://www.ojp.usdoj.gov/bjs/prisons.htm (Accessed October 24, 2009).

4. Officer Down Memorial Page, "Browse by State," http://www.odmp.org/browse.php (Accessed October 24, 2009).

5. Bureau of Justice Statistics, "Deaths in Custody Statistical Tables" http://www.ojp.usdoj.gov/bjs/dcrp/dictabs.htm (Accessed October 24, 2009).

6. *Ibid.*

7. *Ibid.*

8. "Juvenile Justice: A Timeline," New Jersey Juvenile Detention Association, http://www.njjda.org/timeline.htm (Accessed October 24, 2009).

9. "Juvenile Arrests 2007," U.S. Department of Justice, Office of Juvenile Justice and Delinquency Prevention, http://www.ncjrs.gov/pdffiles1/ojjdp/225344.pdf (Accessed October 24, 2009).

10. Guy Cheli, "Sing Sing Prison," New York Corrections History Society, http://www.correctionhistory.org/html/chronicl/state/singsing/cheliindex.html.

11. "History," Eastern State Penitentiary, http://www.easternstate.org/history (Accessed October 24, 2009).

12. Glenn Fowler, "Thomas Murton, 62, a Penologist Who Advocated Reforms, Is Dead," *New York Times,* October 19, 1990.

13. "Texas State Penitentiary at Huntsville," Handbook of Texas Online, http://www.tshaonline.org/handbook/online/articles/TT/jjt1.html (Accessed October 24, 2009).

14. "San Quentin Prison," California Department of Corrections, http://www.cdcr.ca.gov/Visitors/Facilities/SQ.html (Accessed October 24, 2009).

Chapter 5

1. "Mariel Boatlift," GlobalSecurity.org, http://www.globalsecurity.org/military/ops/mariel-boatlift.htm (Accessed October 24, 2009).

2. Robert Pear, "Behind the Prison Riots," *New York Times,* December 6, 1987.

3. *Ibid.*

4. United States White-Slave Traffic Act of 1910 (18 U.S.C. § 2421–2424); National Motor Vehicle Theft Act (18 U.S.C.A. § 2311 et seq.); Federal Kidnapping Act (18 U.S.C. § 1201(a)(1)).

5. Battle of Alcatraz, http://www.alcatrazhistory.com/battle1.htm (Accessed October 24, 2009).

6. Bureau of Justice Statistics, "Prison Statistics," http://www.ojp.usdoj.gov/bjs/prisons.htm (Accessed October 24, 2009); Federal Bureau of Prisons, "About the Bureau of Prisons," http://www.bop.gov/about/index.jsp (Accessed October 24, 2009).

7. Federal Bureau of Prisons, "About the Bureau of Prisons," http://www.bop.gov/about/index.jsp (Accessed October 24, 2009).

8. Bureau of Justice Statistics, "Prison Statistics," http://www.ojp.usdoj.gov/bjs/prisons.htm (Accessed October 24, 2009).

9. "U.S. Disciplinary Barracks," United States Army Combined Arms Center, http://usacac.army.

mil/CAC2/usdb (Accessed October 24, 2009).

10. "List of Military Confinement Facilities," PrisonTalk.com, http://www.prisontalk.com/forums/archive/index.php/t-127953.html (Accessed November 2, 2009).

11. Edna Fernandes, "Supermax Prison, the Alcatraz of the Rockies," *The Times* (London), May 4, 2006.

12. *Ibid.*

13. *Ibid.*

14. Karl Vick, "Isolating the Menace in a Sterile Supermax," *Washington Post,* September 30, 2007.

15. "Executions in the Military," Death Penalty Information Center, http://deathpenaltyinfo.org/executions-military (Accessed October 24, 2009).

16. "Who We Are," Bureau of Indian Affairs, http://www.bia.gov/WhoWeAre/index.htm (Accessed October 24, 2009).

17. "Jails in Indian country, 2007," Bureau of Justice Statistics, http://www.ojp.usdoj.gov/bjs/pub/pdf/jic07.pdf (Accessed October 24, 2009).

18. "Historical Federal Executions," U.S. Marshals Service, http://www.usmarshals.gov/history/executions.htm (Accessed October 24, 2009).

19. "Executions in the Military," Death Penalty Information Center, http://deathpenaltyinfo.org/executions-military (Accessed October 24, 2009).

20. "Facts about the Death Penalty," Death Penalty Information Center, http://www.deathpenaltyinfo.org/documents/FactSheet.pdf (Accessed October 24, 2009).

Chapter 6

1. *The Green Mile*, Internet Movie Database, http://www.imdb.com/title/tt0120689 (Accessed October 24, 2009).

2. "Some Examples of Post-Furman Botched Executions," Death Penalty Information Center, http://www.deathpenaltyinfo.org/some-examples-post-furman-botched-executions (Accessed October 24, 2009).

3. *Ibid.*

4. *Ibid.*

5. *Ibid.*

6. *Ibid.*

7. *Ibid.*

8. *Ibid.*

9. *Ibid.*

10. *Ibid.*

11. *Exodus* 21, 22, and 35; *Leviticus* 19, 20, and 24; *Deuteronomy* 17, 18, 21, and 22.

12. "History of the Death Penalty," Death Penalty Information Center, http://www.deathpenaltyinfo.org/history-death-penalty (Accessed October 24, 2009).

13. *Ibid.*

14. *Ibid.*

15. *Ibid.*

16. "War Crimes Trials," U.S. Holocaust Memorial Museum, http://www.ushmm.org/wlc/article.php?ModuleId=10005140 (Accessed November 2, 2009). "History of the Death Penalty," Death Penalty Information Center, http://www.deathpenaltyinfo.org/history-death-penalty (Accessed October 24, 2009).

17. Thomas Page, "The Real Judge Lynch," *Atlantic Monthly* 88 (December 1901), 731–43.

18. Richard Brown, "The American Vigilante Tradition," in *Violence in America,* Hugh Graham and Ted Gurr, eds. (New York: Bantam, 1969), 154–226.

19. Douglas Linder, "Lynchings by Race and State, 1882–1968," Famous American Trials, http://www.law.umkc.edu/ faculty/projects/ftrials/shipp/ lynchingsstate.html (Accessed October 24, 2009); The Lynching Century, http://www.geoci- ties.com/Colosseum/Base/8507/ NLists.htm (Accessed October 24, 2009).

20. "History of the Death Penalty," Death Penalty Information Center, http://www.deathpenaltyinfo.org/ history-death-penalty (Accessed October 24, 2009).

21. "History of the Death Penalty," Death Penalty Information Center, http://www.deathpenaltyinfo.org/ history-death-penalty (Accessed October 24, 2009).

22. *Ibid.*

23. *Ibid.*

24. *Ibid.*

25. *Ibid.*; FBI Uniform Crime Report 2007, http://www.fbi.gov/ucr/ cius2007/index.html (Accessed October 24, 2009).

26. "History of the Death Penalty," Death Penalty Information Center, http://www.deathpenaltyinfo.org/ history-death-penalty (Accessed October 24, 2009).

27. *Ibid.*

28. The Innocence Project, http:// www.innocenceproject.org/ Content/351.php (Accessed Octo- ber 24, 2009); "History of the Death Penalty," Death Penalty Information Center, http://www. deathpenaltyinfo.org/history- death-penalty (Accessed October 24, 2009); "Illinois Keeping Death Penalty Moratorium," Associated Press, February 6, 2009.

29. "The Execution of Children and Juveniles," Capital Punishment U.K., http://www.capitalpunish- mentuk.org/child.html (Accessed October 24, 2009).

30. "History of the Death Penalty," Death Penalty Information Center, http://www.deathpenaltyinfo.org/ history-death-penalty (Accessed October 24, 2009)

31. *Ibid.*

32. *Ibid.*

33. *Ibid.*

34. "History of the Death Penalty," Death Penalty Information Center, http://www.deathpenaltyinfo.org/ history-death-penalty (Accessed October 24, 2009); "U.S. Execu- tions Since 1976," Clark County Prosecuting Attorney, http://www. clarkprosecutor.org/html/death/ usexecute.htm (Accessed October 24, 2009).

35. "History of the Death Penalty," Death Penalty Information Center, http://www.deathpenaltyinfo.org/ history-death-penalty (Accessed October 24, 2009); Charles Lane, "5-4 Supreme Court abolishes juvenile executions," Washington Post, http://www.washingtonpost. com/wp-dyn/articles/A62584- 2005Mar1.html, (Accessed Octo- ber 27, 2009).

Chapter 7

1. "Paris Hilton Describes Jail Time as 'Traumatic,'" MSNBC, June 27, 2007, http://www.msnbc.msn.

com/id/19467267/ (Accessed October 24, 2009).

2. Michael Y. Park and Jackie Fields, "Khloe Kardashian Recounts Hours in Jail," People. com, http://www.people.com/ people/article/0,,20213731,00.html (Accessed October 27, 2009).

3. "Lindsay Lohan Serves One Day Jail Sentence in 84 Minutes," Fox News, http://www.foxnews.com/ story/0,2933,311886,00.html (Accessed October 27, 2009).

4. "Chris Brown Cops Plea in Assault Case," CBS News, June 22, 2009, http://www.cbsnews.com/ stories/2009/06/22/entertainment/ main5104370.shtml (Accessed October 24, 2009).

5. Bureau of Justice Statistics, "Probation and Parole Statistics," http://www.ojp.usdoj.gov/bjs/ pandp.htm (Accessed October 24, 2009).

6. Florida Department of Corrections, "Timeline," http://www. dc.state.fl.us/oth/timeline/1921. html (Accessed October 24, 2009).

7. William Helmer and Rick Mattix, *Public Enemies* (New York: Checkmark Books, 1998), 254–5, 262–3. 265, 267, 270–1.

8. Dennis Randall, "States with Corporal Punishment in School," Family Education, http://school. familyeducation.com/classroom-discipline/resource/38377.html (Accessed October 24, 2009).

9. "Shaming Criminals: A Good Idea?" (February 17, 1997), BNET, http:// findarticles.com/p/articles/mi_ m0EPF/is_n19_v96/ai_19135802 (Accessed October 24, 2009); Evan Gahr, "Can Shame Tame Cons?" (March 31, 1997), BNET, http://fin-

darticles.com/p/articles/mi_m1571/ is_n12_v13/ai_19241616 (Accessed October 24, 2009); Jeanette Rivas, "Shaming Criminals Straight," *San Jacinto* (Texas) *Times*, April 7, 2008.

10. "Scared Straight! 20 Years Later," Internet Movie Database, http:// www.imdb.com/title/tt0196074 (Accessed October 24, 2009).

11. Anthony J. Schembri, *Scared Straight Programs: Jail and Detention Tours,* Secretary, Florida Department of Juvenile Justice, http://www.djj.state.fl.us/Research/ Scared_Straight_Booklet_Version. pdf (Accessed October 24, 2009).

12. *Ibid.*

13. Amy S. Clark, "Sex Offender Murder Suspect Kills Self," CBS News, April 17, 2006, http://www. cbsnews.com/stories/2006/04/17/ national/main1501271.shtml (Accessed October 24, 2009); Keach Hagey, "Did Sex Offender Listing Lead to Murder?" CBS News, December 10, 2007. http://www.cbsnews.com/ stories/2007/12/10/the_skinny/ main3597422.shtml (Accessed October 24, 2009); "Murder Draws 22-to-Life," *Daily Gazette* (Schenectady, N.Y.), April 3, 2009; "Reward Offered in Murder of Registered Sex Offender," Tampa Bay Online (June 19, 2009), http:// www2.tbo.com/content/2009/ jun/19/191357/reward-sought-murder-registered-sex-offender/ news-breaking (Accessed October 24, 2009).

14. Demian Bulwa and Jaxon Van Derbeken, "Family's Account of Oakland Parolee Who Killed the Four Police Officers," *San Francisco Chronicle,* March 23, 2009;

Andrew Blankstein, "Lovelle Mix-on's Parole Record," *Los Angeles Times,* March 24, 2009.

15. Indiana Code 35-50-6, http://www.in.gov/legislative/ic/code/title35/ar50/ch6.html (Accessed October 24, 2009).

16. Bureau of Justice Statistics, "Probation and Parole Statistics," http://www.ojp.usdoj.gov/bjs/pandp.htm (Accessed October 24, 2009).

17. *Ibid.*

18. *Ibid.*

Chapter 8

1. "Pelican Bay State Prison," California Dept. of Corrections, http://www.cdcr.ca.gov/VISITORS/Facilities/PBSP.html (Accessed October 24, 2009).

2. U.S. Department of Justice press release, May 16, 2002, http://cryptome.org/oz-for-real.htm (Accessed October 24, 2009).

3. *United States v. Jose Ramon Garcia and Edward Michael Powers,* 340 F.3d 1013.

4. Fourth Amendment to the U.S. Constitution.

5. Sixth, Seventh and Eighth Amendments to the U.S. Constitution.

6. *Wilkerson v. Utah* 99 U.S. 130 (1878).

7. "Rights of Inmates," FindLaw.com, http://public.findlaw.com/civil-rights/more-civil-rights-topics/institutionalized-persons-discrimination-more/le5_6rights.html (Accessed October 24, 2009).

8. *Ibid.*

9. "State Felon Voting Laws," ProCon.org, http://felonvoting.procon.org/viewresource.asp?resourceID=286 (Accessed October 24, 2009).

10. Gerald Benjamin and Stephen Rappaport, "Attica and Prison Reform," *Proceedings of the Academy of Political Science* 3 (1974): 203–212.

11. "A Year Ago at Attica," *Time* (September 25, 1972), http://www.time.com/time/magazine/article/0,9171,903593,00.html (Accessed October 24, 2009).

12. "State Felon Voting Laws," ProCon.org, http://felonvoting.procon.org/viewresource.asp?resourceID=286 (Accessed October 24, 2009).

13. *Ibid.*

14. William Farrell, "Rockefeller Lays Hostages' Deaths to Troopers' Fire," *New York Times*, September 17, 1971; "A Year ago at Attica," *Time* Magazine, http://www.time.com/time/magazine/article/0,9171,903593,00.html (Accessed November 2, 2009).

15. PBS, "People & Events: Attica Prison Riot—September 9–13, 1971," PBS.org, http://www.pbs.org/wgbh/amex/rockefellers/peopleevents/e_attica.html (Accessed October 24, 2009).

16. "State Felon Voting Laws," ProCon.org, http://felonvoting.procon.org/viewresource.asp?resourceID=286 (Accessed October 24, 2009).

17. "State Felon Voting Laws," ProCon.org, http://felonvoting.procon.org/viewresource.asp?resourceID=286 (Accessed October 24, 2009).

18. Jeff Manza, Christopher Uggen, and the Sentencing Project, "Felon Voting: Disfranchised Totals by State," ProCon.org, http://felon-voting.procon.org/viewresource.

asp?resourceID=000287 (Accessed October 24, 2009).

19. "Judge Calls Maricopa County Jail Conditions Unconstitutional," American Civil Liberties Union, http://www.aclu.org/prison/conditions/37322prs20081022.html (Accessed November 2, 2009).

20. "ACLU Helps Secure Substantial Settlement for Family of Quadriplegic Left to Die in D.C. Jail," American Civil Liberties Union, http://www.aclu.org/prison/gen/37949prs20081202.html (Accessed November 2, 2009).

21. "ACLU Says Bureau of Prisons Again Attempting to Illegally Ban Religious Material," American Civil Liberties Union, http://www.aclu.org/prison/restrict/39038prs20090317.html (Accessed November 2, 2009).

22. "ACLU Releases Expert's Report on Nightmarish Conditions at Men's Central Jail in Los Angeles," American Civil Liberties Union, http://www.aclu.org/prison/mentalhealth/39363prs20090414.html (Accessed November 2, 2009).

23. "ACLU Says Failure to Properly Administer Medicines at Wisconsin Prison Puts Women's Lives at Risk," American Civil Liberties Union, http://www.aclu.org/prison/medical/38468prs20090123.html (Accessed November 2, 2009).

24. "State's Prison Cable Bill $280,000," *Tulsa World,* December 4, 2008.

Chapter 9

1. Elisabetta Povoledo, "Italian Investigator Says U.S. Agents Left Obvious Clues in Abduction case," *New York Times,* May 29, 2008.

2. Ian Fisher, "Italy Indicts CIA Operatives in '03 Abduction," *New York Times,* February 17, 2007.

3. Ian Fisher, "Italy Prosecutes CIA Agents in Kidnapping," *New York Times,* June 9, 2007; Elisabetta Povoledo, "Kidnapping Trial of CIA Agents Is Suspended by Judge in Italy," *New York Times,* June 19, 2007.

4. Elisabeth Rosenthal, "Italian Trial of CIA Operatives Begins with Torture Testimony," *New York Times,* May 15, 2008; Elisabetta Povoledo, "Milan Judge Says CIA Trial to Continue, with Restrictions," *New York Times,* May 20, 2009.

5. "War Casualties Pass 9/11 Death Toll," CBS News, September 22, 2006, http://www.cbsnews.com/stories/2006/09/22/terror/main2035427.shtml (Accessed October 24, 2009).

6. *Ibid.*

7. Jim VandeHei and Dan Eggen, "Cheney Cites Justifications for Domestic Eavesdropping," *Washington Post,* January 5, 2006.

8. Seema Gupta, "Fitting the Profile after 9/11," Columbia University Journalism School, http://web.jrn.columbia.edu/studentwork/humanrights/muslim-gupta.asp (Accessed October 24, 2009).

9. Bill Miller, "FBI Focus on Terrorism Sidelines Other Categories," *Washington Post,* December 5, 2001.

10. Common Article 3 of the Geneva Conventions, adopted with identical provisions in 1864, 1906, 1929, and 1949.

11. "Guantanamo Bay Detainees," GlobalSecurity.org, http://www.globalsecurity.org/military/facility/guantanamo-bay_detainees.htm

(Accessed October 24, 2009); "Mass Guantanamo Suicide Protest," BBC News, January 25, 2005, http://news.bbc.co.uk/2/hi/americas/4204027.stm (Accessed October 24, 2009); "Triple Suicide at Guantanamo Camp," BBC News, June 11, 2006, http://news.bbc.co.uk/2/hi/americas/5068228.stm (Accessed October 24, 2009).

12. Richard Clarke, *Against All Enemies* (New York: Free Press, 2004), 143–4.

13. Presidential Decision Directive 39, June 21, 1995, http://www.fas.org/irp/offdocs/pdd39.htm (Accessed October 24, 2009).

14. Council of Europe, Resolution 1507, "Alleged Secret Detentions and Unlawful Inter-state Transfers of Detainees Involving Council of Europe Member States," http://assembly.coe.int/Main.asp?link=/Documents/AdoptedText/ta06/ERES1507.htm (Accessed October 24, 2009).

15. Alix Kroeger, "EU to Vote on CIA Flights Report," BBC News, February 14, 2007, http://news.bbc.co.uk/2/hi/6359875.stm (Accessed October 24, 2009).

16. Rebecca Leung, "Abuse of Iraqi POWs by GIs probed," *60 Minutes,* http://www.cbsnews.com/stories/2004/04/27/60II/main614063.shtml, (Accessed October 24, 2009); Seymour Hersh, "Torture at Abu Ghraib," *New Yorker,* http://www.newyorker.com/archive/2004/05/10/040510fa_fact, (Accessed October 24, 2009).

17. "Abu Ghurayb Prison Prisoner Abuse," GolbalSecurity.org, http://www.

globalsecurity.org/intell/world/iraq/abu-ghurayb-chronology.htm (Accessed October 24, 2009).

18. *Ibid.*

19. David Rennie, "Spain Investigates CIA 'Ghost Flights,'" *The Telegraph* (London), November 16, 2005.

20. President's Speech on the Global War on Terror, September 6, 2006, http://www.america.gov/st/texttrans-english/2006/September/20060906155503eaifas0.8319666.html (Accessed October 24, 2009).

21. Scott Shane, David Johnston, and James Risen, "Secret U.S. Endorsement of Severe Interrogations," *New York Times,* October 4, 2007.

22. Josh White, "Interrogated General's Sleeping-Bag Death," *Washington Post,* August 3, 2005.

23. Tim Harper, "Ghost flights over Canada," *Toronto Star*, December 4, 2005.

24. Mona Samari, "Ghost Flights to Black Sites," Amnesty International, http://www.amnesty.org.au/hrs/comments/2185 (Accessed October 24, 2009).

25. "Bush Appoints Texas Ally to Key Post," BBC News, November 10, 2004, http://news.bbc.co.uk/2/hi/4000679.stm (Accessed October 24, 2009); Thalif Deen, "Facing Humiliating Defeat, U.S. Abandons Move to Exempt Troops from War Crimes," Inter Press Service News Agency, June 23, 2004, http://www.commondreams.org/headlines04/0623-08.htm (Accessed October 24, 2009).

26. Bob Woodward, "Detainee Tortured, Says U.S. Official," *Washington Post,* January 14, 2009.

27. Dick Cheney interview, *Face the Nation,* May 10, 2009.

Bibliography

Bruton, James. *The Big House: Life Inside a Supermax Security Prison*. Osceola, Wisc.: Voyageur Press, 2004.

Foucault, Michel. *Discipline & Punish: The Birth of the Prison*. New York: Vintage Books, 1995.

Gottschalk, Marie. *The Prison and the Gallows: The Politics of Mass Incarceration in America*. New York: Cambridge University Press, 2006.

Herivel, Tara, and Paul Wright. *Prison Profiteers: Who Makes Money from Mass Incarceration*. New York: New Press, 2009.

Martin, Tom. *Behind Prison Walls: The Real World of Working in Today's Prisons*. Boulder, Colo.: Paladin Press, 2003.

McShane, Marilyn. *Prisons in America*. El Paso, Texas: LFB Scholarly Publishing LLC, 2008.

Morris, Norval, and David Rothman. *The Oxford History of the Prison*. New York: Oxford University Press, 1997.

Raphael, Steven, and Michael Stoll, eds. *Do Prisons Make Us Safer?: The Benefits and Costs of the Prison Boom*. New York: Russell Sage Foundation Publications, 2009.

Rathbone, Cristina. *A World Apart: Women, Prison, and Life Behind Bars*. New York: Random House, 2006.

Santos, Michael. *Inside: Life Behind Bars in America*. New York: St. Martin's Griffin, 2007.

Further Resources

Books

Christianson, Scott. *Notorious Prisons: An Inside Look at the World's Most Feared-Institutions.* Guildford, Conn.: Lyons Press, 2004.

Earley, Pete. *The Hot House: Life Inside Leavenworth Prison.* New York: Bantam, 1992.

Hassine, Victor, Robert Johnson, and Ania Dobrzanska. *Life Without Parole: Living in Prison Today.* New York: Oxford University Press, 2008.

Talvi, Silja. *Women Behind Bars: The Crisis of Women in the U.S. Prison System.* Jackson, Tenn.: Seal Press, 2007.

Web Sites

Bureau of Justice Statistics
http://www.ojp.usdoj.gov/bjs/prisons.htm

Federal Bureau of Prisons
http://www.bop.gov

Death Penalty Information Center
http://www.deathpenaltyinfo.org

Gangs or Us
http://www.gangsorus.com/prisongangs.html

Index

About the Author

Michael Newton has published 216 books since 1977, with 21 forthcoming from various houses through 2011. His history of the Florida Ku Klux Klan (*The Invisible Empire,* 2001) won the Florida Historical Society's 2002 Rembert Patrick Award for "Best Book in Florida History," and his *Encyclopedia of Cryptozoology* was one of the American Library Association's Outstanding Reference Works in 2006. His nonfiction work includes 13 previous volumes for Facts on File and Checkmark.